GW00775851

Retail Isn't Dead

Matthias Spanke

Retail Isn't Dead

Innovative Strategies for Brick and Mortar Retail Success

palgrave
macmillan

Matthias Spanke
BIG IDEAS Visual Merchandising Inc
Miami, FL, USA

ISBN 978-3-030-36649-0   ISBN 978-3-030-36650-6   (eBook)
https://doi.org/10.1007/978-3-030-36650-6

This Palgrave Macmillan imprint is published by the registered company Springer Nature Switzerland AG.
The registered company address is: Gewerbestrasse 11, 6330 Cham, Switzerland

Preface

Ever since its boom, e-commerce has challenged the processes and services provided by brick-and-mortar retail. Customers love the speed and convenience of online retail, from quick and simple browsing through a vast number of products to payment at the touch of a button and delivery within a very short time to the hassle-free exchange of goods. E-commerce has massively changed the way customers shop. And those people have carried their expectations over to physical retailers. Against this backdrop, however, online business is more than just a competitor and challenge; it has also inspired and innovated the retail business.

If within seconds, customers can navigate through product selections online and find merchandise they are looking for, they will expect that process to be just as easy offline. If they can submit a payment on the web at the touch of a button or via facial recognition, they will hope for the same service in brick-and-mortar retail. Are these expectations too high? No matter how you answer this question, whoever wants to retain customers or attract new ones as a retailer today has to develop strategies to offer the same advantages and even more.

And things get even tougher; the innovation pressure will never end. After all, change paradoxically has come to be the only reliable constant in this globalized and digitalized world. On top of that, this change has happened at a breathtaking speed that, too, has no limits. Retailers may get a little satisfaction from the fact that these new regularities apply to the digital world as well.

But what exactly does online business offer that brick-and-mortar retail usually lacks today?

Let us begin with products: The Internet is never "out of stock." In physical stores, the inventory on hand is limited, while online, there seems to be an unlimited selection. Here, you can navigate through an entire product range with just a few clicks instead of having the tedious task of seeking orientation in a crammed, potentially large store. A hopeless situation for brick-and-mortar retailers? Not at all; international retailers demonstrate solutions for this. Just two successful examples for these adaptations: Macy's demonstrates how you can infinitely extend a product range in the truest sense of the word using virtual reality technology. The Home Depot leads its customers to the merchandise they want via the shortest route using its clever in-store navigation app.

Once a preselection is made, a second or third opinion is often required. Online, these opinions are provided right away as customer reviews, by the dozen at that. Examples from all over the world demonstrate how this can also be done offline in a creative and clever way.

Generally, if you have decided on an item, all you want to do is pay right away. You can do that in the online shop with just a click, fingerprint, or facial recognition. And the merchandise will already be on its way. There is nothing to keep physical retailers from offering the same service: From the checkout kiosk at Zara to Marks & Spencer's "Mobile, Pay, Go" to the "Just Walk Out" technology of Amazon Go, companies demonstrate how that works.

Everyone passes their personal information and shopping habits along—sometimes deliberately but often rather unknowingly. These data are used with artificial intelligence technologies, which enables algorithms to predict the needs of customers. Thus, companies already know today what customers will want tomorrow, even before the latter themselves know it. H&M and other brands demonstrate how that works in brick-and-mortar retail.

But are speed and comfort enough to make a brand really tangible for customers in the physical retail business? Definitely not.

The fact that customers are able to touch, try on, and personally see and compare merchandise in the physical world already presents an advantage and a good start. But why not turn that directly into a brand experience for the customer? At Nike in New York, you can test sneakers on the in-store basketball court and also be guided through user-defined exercises on enormous HD screens. John Lewis & Partners in London fulfill the dream of spending a night at the department store to convince oneself of the quality of the beds there.

To customers, stores are not just places where goods or services are sold. They are—or at least are able to become—part of the community. With co-working spaces like those at the bank branches of Capital One or yoga lessons at sportswear vendor Lululemon, companies demonstrate how they have become a permanent fixture of the community. And thus a permanent fixture in customers' lives.

In terms of sustainability, too, retailers need to change the way they think. In recent years especially, customers have become more aware of the disastrous global development of the environment. More than ever, they expect strategies, commitment, and steps from companies to create long term value by taking into consideration how they operate in the ecological, social and economic environment. That already starts with the shop design. At the IKEA store in London, for example, only renewable resources were used and countless steps taken to successfully make this shop officially the most sustainable store of Great Britain. The number of customers who include an ecological commitment of companies in their purchase decision continues to grow.

There is a large number of steps that can and should be taken to gain competitive advantages in physical retail. The most important and innovative strategies for that are pointed out in this book. These include new brand experiences, potential applications of in-store technologies, sustainability initiatives, and steps to make online advantages available offline. This book is practical and user-oriented, with a lot of tips and over 50 illustrated best-practice examples from a wide variety of industries from all over the world.

Let yourself be inspired and discover new possibilities with which you will be successful in brick-and-mortar retail, now and in the future.

Matthias Spanke
Chief Executive Officer of BIG IDEAS Visual Merchandising Inc, Miami, FL
Chief Executive Officer of BIG IDEAS Visual Merchandising GmbH, Germany
Chief Executive Officer of BIG CAREERS Retail Recruitment, Germany

Acknowledgements

I wish to thank everyone who has supported the realization of this book. Their critique, inspiration, and patience greatly enriched this process both professionally and personally.

I had the great fortune of working with Dr. Kai Kaufmann, and his assistance extended well beyond the regular responsibilities of a lecturer.

Sandi Snively and Ron D'Angelo contributed their enormous expertise to elevate the subject matter of this book. They were tireless and passionate sparring partners as we argued the finer points. Based on her well-known mastery of style, Carla Panzella offered invaluable advice on the translation options for the English book version.

My teams of BIG IDEAS Visual Merchandising and BIG CAREERS Retail Recruitment did a wonderful job backing me up in the daily business of both agencies, which allowed me to give this project the full attention it deserves.

From beginning to end, the entire team of Palgrave Macmillan offered their professionalism, their cooperation, and most importantly, their trust—all of which resulted in ample space for creativity.

Whenever things got rocky, which was often the case in this project, there was always one person who was willing to listen: Gerard Vignuli.

Finally, I would like to express my gratitude to all of the friendly supporters on the part of the companies serving as best-practice examples.

7-Eleven | Sandor Timar (Seven & i Holdings), Yuki Oda (Seven & i Holdings)
7Fresh | Yuchuan Wang (JD.com)
Albert Heijn | Maarten van Tartwijk (Ahold Dellhaize)
Amazon | Laura Gunning
American Girl | Susan A. Jevens

Apple | Martin Kuderna (PRfection), PR-Team (PRfection)
Audi | Susanne Herr, Susanne Killian
b8ta | Brooke Flohr (Bevel PR)
ba&sh | Irene Yuan
Barclays | Eliot Goward
BOTTLETOP | Jessica Jurkschat
Canada Goose | Tobias Woischke
Capital One | Devin Short, Laura Di Lello
Charlotte Tilbury | Amy Nichols, Katie Dobson
DUER Performance | Chanel Pel
Eileen Fisher | Maya Carmosino
Ekoplaza | Diana van den Boomen (UDEA), Steven Ijzerman (UDEA)
H&M | H&M PR-Team
HSBC | Matt Klein
IKEA | Joshua Gbadebo (Hope&Glory PR), Kim Steuerwald
Jelmoli | David Blomerus (Eliane Bachenheimer PR/EBPR), David Zalud
   (Eliane Bachenheimer PR/EBPR)
John Lewis & Partners |Rachael Brown
Kohl's | Melanie Reynolds
LINE FRIENDS | Lena Han, Mina Park (Daniel J. Edelman Holdings, Inc.)
Lowe's | Alice Lee, Gretchen Lopez
Macy's | Christine Olver Nealon, Julie Strider
Marks & Spencer | Emma Brown
MUJI | Anne Robinson (Camron PR Ltd), Helen Cowdry (Camron PR Ltd)
Nike | Anne Eikenboom (Spice PR)
Original Unverpackt | Ria Schäfli
Pepe Jeans | Marta Díaz-Mauriño
Samsung | Isabel Suditsch (Ketchum Pleon GmbH)
Sonos | Breanna Wilson (Daniel J. Edelman Holdings, Inc.), Jenisse Curry
Target | Jacqueline De Buse
The North Face | Michaela Hardy
Uniqlo | Gary Conway (Fast Retailing)
Walmart | Ragan Dickens

Contents

List of Images

Part I

Brand Experience

The digital era has created greater challenges for brick-and-mortar retail. As a result of digitization, customer expectations have changed and increased profoundly in other industries as well. However, the retail sector has been particularly affected. Ironically, retailers are now also starting to face competition in their own backyard. Some online traders are recognizing the advantages of physical retail and opening stores. But everyone is asking the same question: If almost every product that is available worldwide can be found and compared online within seconds, then what advantages are left that make physical retail a convincing option?

Successful retailers have come up with several very good answers to this vitally important question. They create places where customers can explore the brand, enjoy themselves, and experience something new. Why? Because customers are looking for a reason to visit stores. They want a physical experience.

The idea of an in-store customer experience is nothing new. However, the consumer's expectations of how that experience should look have changed. It's no longer sufficient for customers to be greeted upon entering the store, for the goods on display to be changed with each season, and for payment to be hassle-free.

As a retailer, you are facing new challenges. The customer's experience needs to be your main focus. Do consumers enjoy visiting your store? What experiences do you offer them that your competitors and online providers in particular do not? How can you prevent potential disruptive factors in the brand experience?

This chapter will introduce new retail strategies that focus on the customer's experience rather than the actual product. After all, this experience has become the decisive factor when it comes to the success of a brick-and-mortar retail brand.

1

Testing and Playing

A major advantage of physical retail is that the product or service offered can be tested right there and then. This offers the opportunity to physically see it, touch it, and maybe even hear, smell, or taste it. There are often hidden advantages that are not directly obvious to the customer. How can I convince the consumer of the latest technology of running shoes? Or of the sound quality of sound systems being offered? The best way to achieve this is by being able to test it in real life. This requires more than just leaving the product out on display for people to try out. Customers want to have fun and experience something new. They want to know there is added value to making the trip from their computer at home to the physical retail store.

"Try Before You Buy" is the strategy for success. Products or services that are likely to result in increased sales after being tested by a customer are presented to be tried. In that case, it is important to consider which product advantages are not immediately recognizable but nonetheless offer the customer added value. Does the mattress on display offer exceptional comfort and back support? Or is the outdoor clothing wind and waterproof?

Once it has been determined which advantage is to be tested by the consumer, the next question is how to implement it. How can the test be turned into a customer experience? In order to test waterproof jackets, a rain booth could be set up. This would clearly demonstrate under a shower head that the product really is waterproof. The test would work best if the customer was able to try the item out in the rain. In order to enhance the experience even

© The Author(s) 2020
M. Spanke, *Retail Isn't Dead*, https://doi.org/10.1007/978-3-030-36650-6_1

more, a backdrop and the sound of a waterfall in the rain forest could be used to create a tangible setting.

Customers not only want to touch and feel the products; they want to be convinced of their functionality, learn something new, and be entertained. Try passing on specialist knowledge to your consumers during the product test, thus offering added value. While testing running shoes in-store, the customer could, for example, be offered a running analysis. This provides information about the person's foot position and requirements for optimal footwear. Why? Because consumers are inquisitive and require more of their shopping experience. If you meet this need, the store turns into a place for testing and learning.

Encourage the customer to have fun in your store—encourage interaction. Distract stressed consumers from their everyday lives with playful experiences, thus creating a positive brand experience. The cosmetic chain store Sephora in Barcelona gives customers the option of using the escalator or a slide when going downstairs. The slide not only offers some fun but also provides fantastic photo opportunities for social media.

Create areas for testing, playing, and learning where customers can experience your products firsthand. Here, consumers should be entertained and educated. Try to recognize any problems or challenges that customers have when purchasing products and solve these in an innovative and meaningful way. Offer a hassle-free experience that cannot be provided online. Ensure that all actions match the intended brand statement. In-store visits will then result in a successful brand experience.

Call to Action

- Consider which goods or services offer advantages that aren't readily apparent.
- Develop creative and innovative test zones which allow customers to try out these products while at the same time giving them a feeling of being entertained.
- Make sure that while a product is being tested, other areas like playing, learning, and experiencing are also being taken into account.
- Ask yourself whether the action area fits your brand and offers customers a positive brand experience.

DUER Performance: A Denim Playground for Adults

DUER Performance is a Canadian apparel company specializing in functional every-day clothing for men and women who lead active lifestyles. Since its founding in 2013, the headquarters and adjacent flagship store have been situated in Vancouver, Canada. In addition to this location, the company currently has another store in Toronto. It distributes its goods through more than 400 retailers in 150 cities in Canada, the USA, and Europe. DUER currently employs approximately 60 workers.

Image 1.1   DUER Performance. (Source: DUER Performance)

DUER fuses performance and style by combining performance attributes like high-stretch fibers with COOLMAX® for temperature control to create apparel that can handle all you do in a day. Their pants are high-stretch, light-weight, and durable. Other performance features include moisture-wicking, temperature control, and antimicrobial properties. The brand is challenged with communicating all of these product advantages to the customers in an entertaining way and to make them tangible.

In their two physical storefronts, DUER created a Performance Denim Playground for adults. An uncomplicated experience where customers can test the jeans by squatting, stretching, cycling, jumping, and swinging. To achieve this while retaining the existing wooden structure of the building, a tree house was built utilizing the building's high ceilings. It has a net that is suspended 8 feet above the floor and can be used for walking, crawling, or relaxing. There is also a swing and monkey bars. The idea is for customers not only to try on the apparel but also to have fun and experience firsthand how stretchy and comfortable the clothes are.

During a visit to their store, customers are encouraged to jump, climb, and stretch while trying on a pair of DUER pants. Thus, adults get to bring out their inner child while testing out the features of DUER's products. Both new and existing customers are amazed by the Performance Denim Playground. As a result, not only have they increased their brand experience and brand awareness, but also their customer frequency and sales. By introducing this playground, the company created a new kind of shopping experience that allows the product advantages to be tested directly. The store has become an entertaining, active, and experience-oriented retail area.

A further advantage is the fact that the store, along with its experience-oriented course, is directly connected with its headquarters. All head office employees, including the design team, work in the office beside the store and regularly get direct feedback from customers on the Performance Denim Playground.

Nike: In the Test Zone

Nike Inc. is a multinational company with its head office in the greater Portland area of the US State of Oregon. Founded in 1964, the sports brand has almost 1200 stores worldwide and is sold by retail partners in more than 30,000 locations. Nike employs more than 70,000 workers worldwide to design, develop, manufacture, and distribute footwear, apparel, equipment, and accessories. The core target group involves consumers between the ages of 15 and 40.

Image 1.2 Nike. (Source: Nike)

Surveys of Nike customers show: They would like a place where they can play, test products, optimize their own performance, and meet other sports enthusiasts. This is exactly what Nike has done in the New York district of SoHo. Five floors covering an area of over 55,000 square feet beckon people to test, practice, play, and experience.

On the top floor, with a ceiling height of 23 feet, there is a basketball court. As test players throw baskets and test basketball shoes, huge HD screens give them the impression they're playing at the famous basketball courts on the streets of New York. Sensors guide the player through custom exercises on the over-sized screens. Cameras are set up all around the basketball court to capture the action from different vantage points and to show it on the screens in real time during the game.

There are running test zones located on different floors. Here, a treadmill and a huge screen simulate running outdoors. Customers can choose to run for 90 seconds through Central Park or along the water in Battery Park. The treadmill is surrounded by several cameras that record the customer's gait during the run. Store employees analyze the running behavior and are thus able to recommend the most suitable pair of sneakers.

The Nike soccer shoe test area is on the third floor. Here, you will find a large floor area of almost 400 square feet covered with synthetic lawn and surrounded by glass walls. Customers can test soccer shoes and are advised by certified test athletes on specialist topics and product features. In addition, they will find a customization studio, a women's boutique with a personal styling service, and a community meeting point with a seating area.

The whole store is connected to a digital network. The in-store technology is designed in such a way that customers gain new knowledge about their sporting performance. Through their online Nike account, they can access test area film footage and share it on social media. The Nike app is very well designed and uses recorded test data to optimally customize the customer's experience during the next visit to the store. For example, the app not only saves the results of the running analysis but also which shoes the consumer tried on.

Nike offers the customer product experiences that can't be achieved online. These include: going for a virtual run through Central Park, throwing baskets at one of the city's top basketball courts, which has been digitally rendered onto a screen, or a test game in a closed-in soccer field. And there is plenty of specialized knowledge that customers can use to increase their sporting performance in the future. It doesn't matter whether you're training for a marathon, play basketball in your free time, or just love sneakers: This store is worth a trip. Nike has already implemented elements of its successful SoHo project at other locations around the world.

Canada Goose: Ice Age in Hong Kong

Canada Goose Holdings Inc. was founded in Toronto, Canada in 1957. The headquarters of this luxury brand are still located there today. The world's leading manufacturer of high-performance clothing in the luxury sector offers a wide range of jackets, parkas, waistcoats, hats, and gloves. The target group involves women and men between the ages of 25 and 45. Canada Goose has eleven stores on three continents and employs 3800 workers.

Image 1.3 Canada Goose. (Source: Canada Goose)

How do you sell a refrigerator to an Eskimo? This classic question found in handbooks for vendors could be adapted to the next case as follows: How do I test a coat for arctic temperatures in a subtropical place like Hong Kong? Canada Goose took on this challenge. Its answer was to develop a very special test area for stores—the Cold Room. The name is self-explanatory. There is a room integrated into the store that has a temperature of minus 27 degrees Fahrenheit along with ice sculptures. This allows customers to test the products even during the summer months.

The goal was to develop an in-store experience that would not just attract attention but keep the brand authentic. After all, these products basically involve functional outerwear. Canada Goose develops jackets for people who work in the coldest places of the world—the Cold Room enables these jackets to be put to the test. To that end, customers are accompanied into the freezing room by the employees who helped them select the product. If that's not enough, a freezing cold wind can also be generated to enhance the experience. Don't worry: The customers can regulate the airflow themselves. Nobody has to freeze in Hong Kong, even at Canada Goose.

The room is an entertaining and unusual experience that helps customers make informed decisions about their purchases. After all, experimental retail should not only be sensational; more than anything else, it should be useful and relevant. Some customers want to test the arctic temperatures prior to purchasing a jacket. Others want to feel how their bodies react to the temperatures. This generates an opportunity to create a positive brand experience for people who aren't yet customers of Canada Goose but might one day be some.

Long lines of people waiting to try the Cold Rooms are proof of their success, so much so that they have become a selfie magnet. In the meantime, Canada Goose has opened Cold Rooms in half of its stores. They offer entertainment as well as functionality, making them a good example of experience-oriented retail that actually serves a purpose.

Sonos: At Home in the Store

Sonos is an American consumer electronics company that was founded in 2002 in Santa Barbara, California. The headquarters are still located there today. The company is known for its home sound systems with Wi-Fi-enabled smart-speakers. The audio products are sold in a retail store in New York City as well as through 7600 wholesale partners around the world. Sonos currently employs around 1500 workers.

Image 1.4 Sonos. (Source: BIG IDEAS Visual Merchandising Inc)

A challenge for the company was to create a place where customers would have the opportunity to try out the smart-speakers themselves with ease. The idea was to create an atmosphere as if you were testing the products at a friend's house.

The first Sonos flagship store in the New York district of SoHo offers its customers the opportunity to experience just this on an area of almost 4200 square feet. There are seven state-of-the-art Sonos Listening Rooms in the shop. These resemble miniature houses, each furnished and decorated to represent different styles of living. Therefore, almost everyone is able to feel at home in one of them. In each of these houses, every wall represents a different room in order to simulate various listening experiences. Shoppers can retreat into one of these cozy houses, similar to visiting a friend, and try out the smart-speaker systems without any disruption or distraction. At the same time, they will come to realize just how perfectly easy these are to operate.

The Listening Rooms have four layers of acoustic panels and a steel-framed glass door, which ensures that the noise doesn't escape the individual rooms. It has taken a lot of work to develop all this. The initial full-size prototype had to be demolished immediately because it did not offer the desired sound quality and multi-room experience. Today, the Listening Rooms are an integral part of the Sonos retail concept. The store also displays original works of art and decorations created by various artists. In the back is the "Wall of Sound," which is the heart of the store and consists of 297 loudspeakers and acoustic foam.

Customers are not bombarded with product lines in this store, as there are less than ten products on display. They also don't hear different sounds or music coming from every corner. The idea is to replicate that feeling and "a ha" moment when you're in a friend's home and try Sonos for the first time. It's not the store's goal to sell these products on site but rather to assist in the decision-making process of selecting a product and to offer customers a unique experience. The customization helps, as each consumer can play his or her own music in the store and figure out how Sonos would work at home.

b8ta: Test Phase at the Rental Store

b8ta is an American chain store that was founded in California in 2015 and has its headquarters in San Francisco. The company employs around 150 workers and has almost 20 stores that offer retail as a service model. b8ta is a service company providing its store spaces to innovative brands as a showroom.

Image 1.5 b8ta. (Source: b8ta)

Brick-and-mortar retail should be as simple, intelligent, and open as online shopping. This is the credo of b8ta. The company wants to allow customers to personally test the innovative products that are available online. For this purpose, it has implemented the model "Retail as a Service." Brands can easily register online to place products at the store. They then receive detailed analyses of customer interaction and behavior with the products.

It all started with an experimental store in Palo Alto, California and has grown into a nationwide network of shops. The stores are more of a showroom than a sales floor. b8ta offers online traders who have the desire to expand into physical retail, getting the best of both worlds: The products are presented for a limited time period or on a permanent basis, and customers can personally test them prior to purchasing them online.

The stores use software and cameras to seamlessly track customer activity. The advantage for gadget manufacturers is that they learn how customers react to their products. All that is needed for this is a small product selection on the rented shelves of the b8ta stores. Right away, the tenant receives an analysis of collected anonymous data on customer behavior and the interaction with the products at the physical stores.

b8ta does not make any profit from the products sold at its stores. The point isn't making sales in the first place. The equipment manufacturers want their consumers to test their products, receive detailed evaluations, and increase their publicity by exhibiting the devices. b8ta's concept for success is no more and no less than giving the customers the opportunity to try out the product and providing the tenants analyses on customer behavior. In other words: retail as a service.

Samsung 837: Retail-Tainment

Samsung is a global company with its head offices in South Korea. Founded in 1969, the corporation comprises numerous subsidiaries, most of which are grouped under the Samsung brand. There are shops worldwide. In the so-called Samsung Experience Stores, products like virtual reality glasses can be tested and various services can be used. Currently, almost 310,000 workers are employed worldwide by Samsung Electronics.

Image 1.6   Samsung. (Source: BIG IDEAS Visual Merchandising Inc)

This goal may seem paradoxical at first, but Samsung wanted to create a place where customers don't buy products but instead experience the product technology at first hand. The corresponding concept, which Samsung calls "Retail-Tainment," is intended to combine culture, technology, and people in a customer experience. This is exactly what is offered at Samsung 837, the company's flagship store in New York City.

Samsung 837 is also known as "the store that doesn't sell anything." That isn't quite true, as there is definitely something being sold here: an idea of how much pleasure Samsung products have to offer. Thus, employees don't hold standard sales pitches to sell the products to consumers; they are people who are genuine enthusiasts of technology and art. They have a good eye for recognizing who needs help and who would rather just be left alone. In addition, there is a personal advisory service that shows current and new customers how to make the best use of the products.

A main stage dominates the store's entrance area, impressing people with a three-story screen consisting of 96 55-inch flat screens. Numerous music performances take place here every year with top artists like John Legend. If there are currently no artists performing, customers can take a selfie and have it projected onto the huge screen, which is bound to guarantee a lot of Likes.

There are also countless opportunities for virtual-reality experiences on current topics like traveling, sports, music, and seasonal events. If customers can immerse themselves in a virtual world and be transported to any destination, the number of possible experiences seems all but unlimited. In addition to interactive stations that change on a regular basis, the store has a radio, music, and DJ studio that acts as an interactive hosting space for radio broadcasts, podcasts, DJ sets, live recordings, and interviews with celebrities.

The lounge and playroom can be found on the top floor. Both are comfortable places for relaxing and trying out Samsung equipment. In the lounge, you can work on your own computer or simply imagine how nice this 60-inch flat-screen TV would look at home. The adjacent, fully equipped kitchen has the latest appliances as well as a fridge that is connected to the internet. Thus, while out grocery shopping, you can use your smartphone to see what is in the fridge at home and check what is missing. There is a café next to the kitchen. Coffee, donuts, and cookies are obviously the only things that can really be purchased in this store. Of course, you can pay here using Samsung Pay.

A lot of what is installed in this store is designed so that visitors can record images and videos and share these with friends on social media. Therefore, the success of the store is not measured by its sales figures but rather by its social media presence. Samsung 837 is a smart retail concept that unites cultural events and product experiences on a technical playground.

Apple: Apple of Knowledge

Apple Inc. is a global technology company with his main office in Cupertino, California. The company, which was founded in 1976, develops and sells entertainment electronics, computer software, and online services. Apple has the highest turnover among technology companies and is the third-largest mobile phone manufacturer in the world. The product range includes smartphones, tablets, computers, portable media players, smartwatches, earbuds, smart-speakers, software, online services, and payment systems. The first of more than 500 stores on five continents was opened in 2001. Currently, the company employs more than 100,000 workers on a full-time basis.

Apple is a leading developer of innovative and user-friendly computer products, and the company is just as innovative in its approach to retail. Its maxim: Apple stores should be a place to learn and meet like-minded people. Today, Apple connects its products and services almost seamlessly. Customers can test products on site and gain the necessary know-how from professionals. The biblical "apple from the tree of knowledge," which is reflected in Apple's logo, makes double sense at the stores.

Consumers invest a lot of time and effort in researching their purchases; they collect information that is important to them. Apple figured that retailers could provide this information, not in the form of a marketing campaign but as a free service offer. The training concept "Today at Apple" offers precisely this service—practical knowledge for using Apple technology. Highly qualified team members share their expert knowledge with Apple customers at more than 50 events in free store sessions.

"Today at Apple" is aimed at customers of all ages, and its educational content covers all levels of difficulty. In the "Music Lab for Kids," six to twelve-year-olds find out how to produce a title song for their favorite show using the program GarageBand on the iPad. In an app session, adults learn how to develop and implement an app idea using Keynote. There is a wide variety of courses on photography, video, music, coding, art, and design. Naturally, all courses focus exclusively on features of Apple products.

The Apple education program is designed to make it easier for customers to use Apple technology. We have probably all experienced the frustration of technology taking us for a ride, when it seems to do everything but work. Thus, the primary goal here is to share new, practical knowledge, as customers want to learn something new that takes their knowledge to the next level. In order to achieve this, they would like the support of professionals. This is the secret to creating enthusiasm and inspiring and retaining customers.

Bibliography

Apple. 2017. "Today at Apple" Bringing New Experiences to Every Apple Store. https://www.apple.com/newsroom/2017/04/today-at-apple-bringing-new-experiences-to-every-apple-store/.
———. 2019. Apple Announces New Today at Apple Sessions. https://www.apple.com/newsroom/2019/01/apple-announces-new-today-at-apple-sessions/.

B8ta. Our Mission: Retail Designed for Discovery. https://b8ta.com/about-us.

Brown, Matthew. Echo Chamber. 'Samsung 837, New York'. https://echochamber.com/article/samsung-837-new-york/.

Danziger, Pamela N. 2018. Canada Goose Opens The Cold Room So Customers Can Experience Its Warmth. https://www.forbes.com/sites/pamdanziger/2018/09/15/canada-goose-opens-the-cold-room-so-customers-can-experience-its-warmth/#52f2290059f8.

DUER Performance. Vancouver Flagship Store. https://shopduer.com/pages/vancouver.

Herrera, Sara. 2019. Retail as a Service – Experiences Statt Umsätze! https://www.handelskraft.de/2019/08/retail-as-a-service-experiences-statt-umsaetze-5-lesetipps/.

Howland, Daphne. 2019. Store Concept b8ta Expands into Fashion, Lifestyle. https://www.retaildive.com/news/store-concept-b8ta-expands-into-fashion-lifestyle/565184/.

Keh, Pei-Ru. 2016. Sounds Like Home: Sonos Opens Its First Flagship Store in New York. Wallpaper*. https://www.wallpaper.com/design/sonos-opens-a-ground-breaking-flagship-store-in-nyc.

NIKE. 2016. First Look: Inside Nike Soho. https://news.nike.com/news/nike-soho-first-look.

PRNewswire. 2016. First Sonos Retail Flagship Brings Music Home to New York City. https://www.prnewswire.com/news-releases/first-sonos-retail-flagship-brings-music-home-to-new-york-city-300296998.html.

SAMSUNG. 2016. Samsung 837 Opens Its Doors in the Heart of NYC Marking the First-of-Its-Kind Cultural Destination, Digital Playground and Marketing Center of Excellence. https://news.samsung.com/global/samsung-837-opens-its-doors-in-the-heart-of-nyc-marking-the-first-of-its-kind-cultural-destination-digital-playground-and-marketing-center-of-excellence.

———. 2018. Samsung 837 2nd Anniversary Marks Rise of "Retailtainment". https://news.samsung.com/us/samsung-837-2nd-anniversary-marks-rise-retailtainment/.

———. About Us > Overview. https://news.samsung.com/global/overview.

Stewart, Megan. 2017. Dish & Duer Relaunches Gastown with Indoor Performance Playground. https://www.vancourier.com/living/dish-duer-relaunches-in-gastown-with-indoor-performance-playground-photos-1.20684851.

Trotter, Kate. 2017. An Insider Look at Dish & DUER – The Retail Company with the In-store Playground. http://www.insider-trends.com/an-insider-look-at-dish-duer-the-retail-company-with-the-in-store-playground/.

2

Paid Experience

Retailers are looking for opportunities to expand the influence of their brands. They have to come up with authentic new ways of connecting their brand with customers. In this chapter, you'll find out how to create brand experiences paid for by customers. Brand experiences that go above and beyond the normal core business. But which business areas outside your own core business would be suitable for this, and which ones can you really create a new and authentic brand experience with?

Diversification is the keyword here. It describes a growth strategy in which products, services, and markets are added to the company's core business. Diversification can lead to a new brand experience. Magazines open their own food markets, and fitness studios bring the brand name into a new area of their customers' lives with fitness boutique hotels.

When experimenting with new categories or industries to expand business, the first thing you need to ask yourself is which products or services have the potential to create a new brand experience for customers. This could be a completely new industry like a barbershop that opens a whisky lounge as part of expanding its brand. Or new product development that offers further customer benefits in addition to the new brand experience. With the introduction of Apple's Titan credit card, customers are offered an experience that ranges from product selection to the final purchase process. Alternatively, business can be expanded through related products. For example, a fragrance store can also offer beauty treatments as a way to broaden the brand experience. Something else to consider would be an additional location where your own products can be presented and experienced. This could be a furniture

© The Author(s) 2020
M. Spanke, *Retail Isn't Dead*, https://doi.org/10.1007/978-3-030-36650-6_2

store, for example, that now equips the hotel of the same brand with its own furniture.

It's vitally important that the expansion of the brand through a paid event actually represents a customer experience. If a sports brand opens a café, then it shouldn't just be a showroom for its own products. Positioning the products in a clever way is crucial for its success, but this should only be part of the concept. It is important that the concept is not interchangeable, that it represents an experience, and that it reflects the brand in its many different aspects. In the case of the café, it covers the customer's experience from entering to leaving the room; it ranges from the furnishing to the music to the employees.

In order to create a new customer experience, brands need to expand what they offer beyond products. After all, a brand is far more than just the sum of its products. A brand is an experience, and customers are happy to pay for such an experience. In addition to a new source of income, this also offers a great opportunity for strong customer retention. However, be careful not to venture too far from your core business and out of your comfort zone, as expanding into new business areas will inevitably take up management time and thus distract attention from other parts of your business that currently ensure the company's success.

Call to Action

- Consider which related market segments your product fits into or which products you can use to enhance your brand experience.
- Analyze which partnerships you can utilize for competency, location, or their partner network.
- Make sure that the entire customer experience is an event that matches your brand.

Tiffany & Co.: Breakfast at Tiffany's

Founded in 1837, the company Tiffany & Co.—better known as Tiffany's—is an American luxury jewelry retailer with its headquarters in New York City, USA. In addition to jewelry and sterling silver, the 300 stores worldwide also sell porcelain, crystal, fragrances, watches, and accessories. They employ more than 14,000 workers.

Even though Tiffany & Co. is a classic store, it isn't immune to the changing retail landscape. Declining numbers of marriages don't make the business any easier, either. Apart from that, it is important to always be on the lookout for new and exciting opportunities and concepts to retain and win customers. Many retailers have been running cafés for decades to offer an additional service and increase customer frequency. But there is probably no other brand that can stage a café as a new brand experience as well as Tiffany's did.

It's been more than 50 years since Audrey Hepburn, acting as Holly Golightly, looked yearningly at the glistening window display of the noble jeweler while eating a croissant. Ever since then, the film "Breakfast at Tiffany's" has been part of the brand. Today, it's no longer necessary to stand in front of the window with a paper bag in your hand, as Tiffany & Co. has its own café. With the Blue Box Cafe on New York's famous Fifth Avenue, the location of the original film, new target groups are being introduced to the brand. Those who can't afford a diamond ring may treat themselves to the "Breakfast at Tiffany" for 29 dollars to immerse themselves somehow in the glamorously romantic world of Tiffany.

In the film, coffee was served in paper cups. However, in the current era of sustainability considerations, things are different. Tiffany's offers its customers the chance to have breakfast all day—party girl Holly was never an early riser. On the fourth floor of the luxury jeweler, where home accessories can be found, is the café, which directly overlooks Central Park. The room, chairs, and dishes are all in Tiffany's blue tones, and the walls are fitted with display cases. The café provides its visitors with a contemporary luxury experience and enables a special, new brand experience.

Of course, social media was not forgotten. There are photo-friendly spots everywhere, all displaying the brand colors of blue and white. No matter what income you have, the Blue Box Cafe offers customers access to the glamorous world of Tiffany & Co.—even if only for a selfie.

American Girl: Wellness for the Doll

American Girl is a series of 18-inch dolls released by Pleasant Company in 1986. Nowadays, American Girl is a subsidiary of Mattel with its headquarters in Wisconsin, USA. In 1998, the first retail store "American Girl Place" was opened in Chicago. There are 17 such stores in the USA, and retail partners in Canada, and the United Arab Emirates. The company employs around 1700 workers, doubling this number during the Christmas season.

Image 2.1 American Girl. (Source: BIG IDEAS Visual Merchandising Inc)

American Girl discovered experience-based retail over 20 years ago. Up until 1998, the dolls were only available via mail order. But even then, the stores were more than just a salesroom. The dolls were shown in action. There were bistros, doll salons, a doll hospital, and a range of exclusive products. Then and now, a visit to an American Girl Place store was supposed to be more than just a place for purchases; it was supposed to be a brand experience for American Girl fans.

To this day, the company has remained true to the product concept. The dolls present eight to twelve-year-old girls of different ethnicities. They are sold with accompanying books, which are written from the girls' perspective. A variety of clothes and accessories is available as well. A new service has been added for ordering tailor-made dolls with individual looks and items of clothing according to your wishes.

American Girl has used the "paid experience" in almost every conceivable area to create an all-inclusive brand experience in its stores. Should an "accident" happen, the American Girl doll hospital experts are there to help. From a thorough cleaning to the "big operation," the "doctors" treat every doll. There are even hearing aids available for the little ladies at a price of 14 dollars. At the American Girl hairdressing salon, young customers can choose a style for their dolls in lookbooks and watch how the dolls are transformed in front of their eyes. You can also book a "Spa Deluxe Day" for your doll, which encompasses a manicure made up of self-adhesive fingernails or earrings.

At the American Girl restaurant, both young and old are served brunch, lunch, afternoon tea, or dinner at tiny tables naturally set for both the girls and their dolls. In addition, a reservation can be made for various birthday party packages or VIP shopping evenings. And if all that isn't enough, the American Girl hotel package can be booked. Accommodation is offered at a partner hotel where the doll is treated as a VIP and sleeps in an exclusive doll bed. Sounds crazy? For sure. But the little ladies love it.

This is how American Girl offers every little girl the perfect day. An experience that is well paid for and inspires not only lifelong memories but enduring brand loyalty as well, hopefully also for these children's children in the future.

MUJI: Eating, Sleeping, Shopping

This company, founded in 1980, has its headquarters in Tokyo, Japan. MUJI is derived from the Japanese words Mujirushi Ryohin and means "non-branded quality goods." Accordingly, the company has set itself the goal of manufacturing and selling simple, inexpensive, and high-quality products. There are more than 900 MUJI stores worldwide that carry a wide range of household goods, apparel, and food. On average, the stores are 2150 square feet in size. MUJI considers all that relate to MUJI philosophy to be their customers. MUJI employs more than 19,000 workers worldwide.

Image 2.2 MUJI. (Source: Ryohin Keikaku)

Hotels are the new showrooms for the retail business. Stores selling furniture and household goods are increasingly moving into the hotel industry. The reason: It is a perfect place where customers can interact with the brand. For MUJI, offering its own hotels presents the opportunity for a seamless brand experience. The Japanese retailer's minimalist and linearly designed products optimally match the esthetics of our time and the wishes of modern travelers.

The interior esthetics of MUJI hotels are reserved, minimalist, and functional, which is exactly what the retailer is known for in its other product segments. The interior design captivates with its linear design, which is even reflected in the texture of the towels and the arrangement of sockets and light switches. Light-colored wood furniture is combined with neutral textiles and green plants to create a calming appeal.

There are currently three MUJI hotels: in Shenzhen, Beijing, and Tokyo. The latter was opened in Spring 2019 in the Ginza district. Ginza is the center for luxury shopping in Tokyo. On the top floor of the MUJI flagship store the hotel is located. The MUJI Ginza flagship store and MUJI HOTEL together provide an environment where customers can experience the philosophy of MUJI. The difference is that in the hotel rooms customers can close the door behind them and test the products in peace as if they were in their own home.

Almost everything on display in the hotel rooms can also be purchased by the guests. From the award-winning wall-mounted CD player to the feather pillows and covers to toothbrush holders, cotton swabs, and slippers. Even if these are all MUJI products, their integration is always subtle and well thought out. MUJI offers its customers a comprehensive brand experience, for a fair price at that. Exactly what the brand stands for: simple, inexpensive, and high-quality.

Bibliography

American Girl. Explore What's in Store. https://www.americangirl.com/retail/.

McDonough, Megan. 2018. Breakfast at Tiffany Is Served at the Jeweler's Flagship Fifth Avenue Store. https://www.washingtonpost.com/lifestyle/travel/finally-breakfast-at-tiffany-is-served-at-the-jewelers-flagship-fifth-avenue-store/2018/10/11/7ee35004-cbd4-11e8-920f-dd52e1ae4570_story.html.

Ryohin Keikaku Co., Ltd. 2019. MUJI Hotel Ginza. https://ryohin-keikaku.jp/eng/news/2019_0319_e.html.

Tiffany & Co. 2017. Tiffany & Co. Opens New Home & Accessories Floor and Blue Box Café at Its Fifth Avenue Flagship Store. http://press.tiffany.com/News/NewsItem.aspx?ID=324.

3

Pop-Up Shop

Customers want to see and experience new things in retail. They want to be surprised, inspired, and encouraged. This can be achieved through products or experiences that the customer doesn't expect from the store. However, how can a company ensure in practice that its customers are continually being offered something new? A possible solution is a pop-up shop, which is an area of the store that is used to display products or services for a limited period of time. Sure, this is nothing new. But what is new is the fact that pop-up shops are an integral part of the retail strategy.

There can be one or more areas in the store that are used either permanently for alternating pop-up shops or erected and dismantled with complete flexibility as required. It is always important that the areas clearly stand out from the rest of the store. They offer every conceivable scope to be creative and create truly new experiences. This is a great advantage, as "new" draws customers. The second great advantage is that what is being offered is only available for a limited time. This is a thought no doubt everyone can relate to: If you know a product won't be available much longer, you are more likely to purchase it faster.

Pop-up shops are also an excellent way to test something new. That can be new brands, concepts, products, or extensions of your product range. If, for example, you are considering introducing a new product, then a pop-up shop is an optimal way to do a test run. Here, you can talk directly with customers and get feedback. Because of the size and the fact that the pop-up shop already looks different than the rest of the store, adjustments based on customer feedback can be made quickly and without a problem. The "test lab pop-up shop" can thus deliver valuable figures and customer feedback on new products in a short time.

© The Author(s) 2020
M. Spanke, *Retail Isn't Dead*, https://doi.org/10.1007/978-3-030-36650-6_3

Another alternative for using pop-up shops is to partner with companies that either serve the same customers as you or promise to expand your own customer base. With pop-up retail, you can offer products or services that may not be possible without the partner's expertise. Or you rent out the area at a profit. It's not unusual for brands to be willing to pay for more presence in physical retail stores or to assume the costs for the design, production, and implementation of a pop-up shop. It's always worth talking to your own product suppliers about it. A partnership is possible in either direction. Either you can erect a pop-up in your own store, or you find partners that allow you to offer your products in a special area of their store. In addition to retail areas, events are also suitable for pop-up shops.

Maybe, however, you would also like to present a curated selection of products from your store. The pop-up shop concept is best in this situation as well. Products for a theme, trend, or even for a product group are possible. Take Halloween, for example: Everything solely to do with trick-or-treating is combined, from costumes to sweets to decorations. Current trends are also suitable for creating a pop-up. Compile a selection of products that currently have the greatest customer interest.

It doesn't matter which product range you create; you need high customer frequency for your concept to be successful. One way of achieving this is to use social media on a local level. The correct hashtags and well-planned events will lure customers into the store to then gain a new brand experience in your pop-up shop.

Pop-up shops can be a permanent strategy for your retail business. They offer customers a changing array of new products and experiences. They offer you a testing area with direct customer feedback, which can be very valuable for corporate decisions. Thus, pop-ups work well as a changing test area because they offer a high degree of flexibility and speed, and with a little creativity, they can also be implemented at a reasonable cost.

Call to Action

- Select brands, concepts, products, partners, or themes for your pop-up shops in such a manner that they offer your customers a new brand experience.
- Position the shop in an area of your store that is highly frequented and clearly visible.
- Be creative with the design and don't be afraid to make it look completely different from the rest of the store one time.
- Talk to your customers and take steps directly to ensure maximum success from the pop-up shop.

Foot Locker: Sneakers on Tour

Foot Locker, Inc. is a global retail chain for athletically inspired shoes and apparel that was founded in 1974. The company's main office is in Manhattan in New York City, USA. There are over 3200 stores worldwide in 27 countries with almost 50,000 employees. The product range includes sneakers, apparel, and accessories, with almost 70 percent of the products coming from Nike. Since 2007, the House of Hoops by Foot Locker is available as independent stores or shop-in-shops. These spaces offer a range of premium sneakers and apparel from Nike, Jordan, and Converse.

Tens of thousands of fans who support basketball, a national sport of the US, gather at large events during the US basketball season. A large percentage of them fall exactly under the House of Hoops target group. Instead of trying hard to get all these people into the stores, you can just do the opposite and bring the store to the fans. That is exactly what Foot Locker has done with the "HOH Courtside" pop-up.

At the start of the 2018/2019 NBA season, Nike and Foot Locker entered into a joint venture. Together they started a pop-up tour of the USA's most important basketball events. "HOH Courtside" offered exclusive product launches, sneakers from Nike, Jordan, and Converse, as well as Nike sportswear and NBA-licensed articles. A highlight was the customization area where athletes and fans could make the products unique. Thus, fans could completely immerse themselves in the NBA event even before and after the games, making it a memorable experience.

The pop-up was designed out of several large dice, each eight square feet in size, that could be arranged individually. It was pivotal that all the elements could be transported without any problems. The pop-up was made in less than three weeks. It consisted of steel substructures with a wooden frame, LED lighting, integrated partition walls, and graphic elements.

The "HOH Courtside" pop-up tour was a huge success. Tens of thousands of people were able to gain a new brand experience in that short time. Countless pairs of shoes were individualized, and some products were completely sold out quickly. Even the social media strategy was a success. The pop-up was strongly represented on social platforms, as customers took a lot of photos and then shared them.

John Lewis & Partners: A Night in the Department Store

John Lewis & Partners is a British chain of luxury department stores. Since the first store was opened on London's Oxford Street in 1864, another 50 stores have been opened in Great Britain. Today, the company employs over 28,100 employees, who at the same time are regarded as partners. Fashion, cosmetics, furniture, and house-hold goods are offered on the sales areas averaging 132,000 square feet in size. The core target group involves women and men between the ages of 35 and 44.

Image 3.1 John Lewis & Partners. (Source: John Lewis & Partners)

In-store health and wellness concepts have been very popular with consumers for years. There is a good reason for this, as in our fast-moving, global world, peaceful moments are becoming increasingly more valuable. No wonder that strategies related to the merchandise category of sleep are gaining more importance. This theme ranges from mattresses to bedding to pajamas and night care products. John Lewis & Partners teamed up with the lifestyle blog "The Midult" and developed the pop-up "The Lying Down Club" with a sleep-related product range.

The bed department on the third floor of the London flagship store was transformed into a sleeping room without further ado. During the pop-up campaign that ran from 6pm until 8pm, customers were given the chance to take a relaxing nap. Upon their arrival, they received a cozy bathrobe, slippers to feel comfortable in, headphones with noise suppression, and an eye mask like on a plane. Visitors could get a massage from spa experts or take a short trip to the Maldives with virtual-reality glasses. Those who just wanted to have some peace and quiet could relax in the freshly made-up beds.

The two-hour sessions had to be booked online in advance; the target group with sleep deprivation and the need for a time-out is huge. Up to two people could make themselves comfortable in a double room for 15 pounds, with snacks and all services included. The two-day pop-up event attracted a lot of attention, with media all over the world reporting on the horizontal brand experience in the middle of the city.

Jelmoli: Destination to Innovation

The fashion store Jelmoli was founded in Zurich in 1833. Today, it is the largest premium department store in Switzerland with around 1000 brands being offered on six floors and 258,000 square feet of sales area. There are more than 1000 people employed at this location. The product range includes apparel, accessories, cosmetics, jewelry, and furnishings. Additionally, there are restaurants and a food market. It is aimed at the core target group of women and men between the ages of 25 and 55.

Image 3.2 Jelmoli. (Source: Jelmoli)

Jelmoli set itself the goal of creating a pop-up shop for fans of smart gadgets and technical innovations. To that end, a partnership was entered into with the British start-up company Smartech in 2018, which led to the opening of the pop-up "Destination to Innovation."

What made Smartech so attractive as a partner? The company tracks down technical innovations worldwide and helps inventors tell their story. Only the best products with exciting visions are included in the product range, which nowadays can be found in the largest department stores of Europe. At Jelmoli, Smartech presents exclusive lifestyle gadgets. These include picture frames that adjust the picture on a whim; snapchat glasses that capture every moment on and in water and then post the pictures to social networks; drones that fly independently and follow the user; playful feeding and video systems for dogs; and much more.

All equipment can be tested directly in-store. In addition, there are interesting videos and background information on the displays. For Jelmoli customers, the constantly changing innovative products are an exciting extension of the product range. The strategy is obviously working, as the success of the pop-up shop made "Destination to Innovation" an integral part of the assortment.

Nordstrom: Pop-in Boutique

Nordstrom Inc. is an American luxury department store chain with its headquarters in Seattle in the US State of Washington. Founded in 1901, the company employs over 70,000 workers and has nearly 400 stores in the USA and Canada. Nordstrom carries apparel, accessories, shoes, cosmetics, and fragrances. At select stores, there are also departments for wedding attire and furnishings.

As early as several years ago, Nordstrom developed a pop-up strategy to regularly offer customers unique experiences. Younger customers were being targeted here as well, and people who normally might not shop at Nordstrom were expected to visit the store. The intention was to deliberately disrupt the store's uniformity and create a permanent pop-up area with a boutique-like character that was typical of an independent retailer.

Pop-in@Nordstrom has been in place since the end of 2013, offering an on-going range of themed pop-up shops. The assortment changes every four to six weeks in order to continually offer customers new interesting experiences as reasons to return. The concept offers two variants. The first is a pop-up shop with a theme range made up of various carefully curated product categories and brands. The second is a pop-up shop from a partnership with just one brand. In the latter case, an up-and-coming designer is offered an opportunity to showcase him or herself in brick-and-mortar retail.

The pop-up products are handpicked and tell a consistent story. They involve articles that normally aren't found in Nordstrom stores. Thus, the average customers at the shopping center may be introduced to something new. This ranges from emerging labels to collectibles to luxury articles. The concepts take into account any current trends. The plan is to offer customers exactly those products that Nordstrom team members themselves may be enjoying now.

The pop-up shops are designed individually for each theme. This arouses curiosity and surprises customers over and over again. It all happens very quickly, taking only a few months from inspiration through product selection and purchase to implementation at the stores.

Macy's: Retail as Service

The American department store chain Macy's was founded by Roland Hussey Macy in New York in 1858. Since 2015, it has been the largest department store chain in the USA in terms of retail sales. With 1,250,000 square feet of sales space, the New York flagship store is even one of the largest department stores in the world. Around 130,000 workers are employed at the company's headquarters and the approximately 640 branches in the USA, Puerto Rico, and Guam, 38 Bloomingdale's stores and nearly 170 Bluemercury locations. The product range includes fashion, accessories, jewelry, cosmetics, fragrances, kitchen utensils, and furnishings. Macy's stores offer something for the whole family, but the main target group involves middle-class women between the ages of 16 and 34.

Image 3.3 Macy's. (Source: Macy's)

Macy's has set new standards with its pop-up concept The Market @ Macy's. At select stores, areas are made available that are leased as pop-up spaces. The strategy is called "retail as service." It offers the company frequently changing new products for its customers, which results in an increase in customer frequency and additional income through rent and other services.

The service is aimed at brands wanting to test new concepts in physical retail stores, but without the high time and cost expenditure involved in setting up an own store. The areas start at around ten 100 square feet and can be rented for one to three months. They are situated in prime store locations with high customer frequency. The tenants renting the spaces keep all the income. A very practical feature for the tenant is the fact that Macy's full-service program includes set-up according to the respective brand vision and support for the pop-up area from trained sales staff. In addition, the tenant receives a comprehensive data analysis, such as the daily sales figures, visitor numbers, and conversion rate.

To kick off its first Christmas season The Market @ Macy's entered into a partnership with Facebook. Products from 150 e-commerce brands advertised on the social media platform were sold at the shops. The assortments offered range from clothing, accessories, and beauty to home decor, technology, and much more.

This concept has a lot of advantages for Macy's. Surplus areas are used to offer customers a frequently changing range of products. In addition to rental income, Macy's gains insight into customer preferences and buying behavior with respect to the new products.

Bibliography

Jelmoli. Smartech. https://www.jelmoli.ch/smartech-pop-up.
Macy's. Introducing the Market @ Macy's. https://www.themarketatmacys.com/about.
Mayne, Sarah. 2018. House of Hoops Courtside. Satis&fy. http://satis-fy-usa.com/hoh-courtside-2018.
———. 2019. House of Hoops – Courtside. Satis&fy. http://satis-fy-usa.com/blog/tag/footlocker.
Nordstrom. 2017. Olivia Kim Brings The Korean Brands You Need to Know to Nordstrom. https://press.nordstrom.com/news-releases/news-release-details/olivia-kim-brings-korean-brands-you-need-know-nordstrom.
Rivkin, Annabel. 2017. The Lying Down Club: Getting Tucked Up in the Bed Department of John Lewis?. https://www.tatler.com/article/the-lying-down-club-sleepover-john-lewis.
Salpini, Cara. 2018. A Look Inside Macy's New Retail Strategy. https://www.retail-dive.com/news/a-look-inside-macys-new-retail-strategy/543073/.
Settele, Claude. 2018. Jelmoli eröffnet einen Pop-up-Store für ausgefallene Lifestyle Gadgets. https://bellevue.nzz.ch/auto-gadgets/jelmoli-eroeffnet-pop-up-store-fuer-ausgefallene-lifestyle-gadgets-ld.1427283.

4

Community Hub

In this day and age, many people suffer from loneliness or even social isolation, which is a paradox in light of the extent to which we are networked with "friends" on social platforms, often with hundreds of them. But according to experts, this constant online connection promotes the decline of real relationships. In Great Britain, there has even been a Ministry for Loneliness since 2018. Young people in particular yearn to belong to analog communities. This provides a great opportunity for retail businesses because stores can become part of a community, not just a place that displays and sells products. Instead, they can become places where people are able to come together and exchange ideas. Sociologists refer to this as the "third places," in other words, places that are visited between home and work for the purpose of social interaction. This almost sounds like the good old community centers—quite, as bizarre as it may sound. But how does something become such a community hub?

With declining retail sales, stores need to adjust their inventory to match their sales, which often leads to empty spaces in salesrooms. These unused spaces offer retailers the opportunity to create a so-called community gathering place, that is, a meeting place.

Create an area where customers are welcome to stay for an extended period of time. Offer people not only your products but also opportunities for leisure activities. Offer cultural events or create a co-working space. Social spaces and the integration into communities create more customer frequency, loyalty, and often additional income sources.

In order to create a community gathering place, you need to gain and maintain customers' trust. What is the best way to gain their trust? By giving

© The Author(s) 2020
M. Spanke, *Retail Isn't Dead*, https://doi.org/10.1007/978-3-030-36650-6_4

your customers the feeling with every activity of yours that you don't just want to sell them something.

Consumers need to have a good reason to want to meet in a store. This could be a weekly yoga class at a brand of sportswear, or a DJ who plays in the lounge area of a young-fashion retailer every Saturday. Events not only draw local crowds but also offer customers the chance for social networking. That is exactly how a retailer establishes itself as an important part of the community.

One strategy can involve offering customers services that pertain to their everyday needs. This could be an in-store restaurant or maybe a stylish coin-operated laundromat at a denim retailer. If local conditions allow, an area can be leased for regular events, thus turning the community hub into a brand experience.

Implementing a co-working area is also a good option for establishing a community. More and more employees are requesting flexible working hours, and more and more companies are offering different solutions for this. One response involves the home office, which is becoming more and more popular. However, one of the biggest challenges of working from home is the lack of companionship gained through colleagues and teams. This explains the enormous increase in co-working spaces that has been observed over the last few years. But how do you create a meeting place for young employees and freelancers with relatively little effort? What you need are good seating options that are also suitable for groups, a high-speed internet connection, and events that suit the brand and the target group.

Provide regular or long-term reasons why your store should be visited as a community gathering place. As a "third place" that offers customers real added value. Community events that contribute to a memorable brand experience, build trust, and aren't just aimed at selling your merchandise.

Call to Action

- Identify an area in your store where the community can meet on a regular basis.
- Consider which benefits and added value you want to offer your community that will also create an incentive for visits in the long run.
- Analyze which events, service offers, or even partners are suitable for establishing a community gathering place.
- Build customer trust with the community events. Make sure that your products are part of the events but not the only part.

Lululemon: In the Om Club

Founded in 1998, Lululemon Athletica Inc. is a Canadian sportswear retailer. The company has its head office in Vancouver and has over 400 stores in North America, Asia, Europe, and Oceania. More than 13,000 employees work for the yoga-inspired company. Performance shirts, shorts, pants, as well as lifestyle apparel and yoga accessories for women and men are offered at the stores.

"Sweat. Grow. Connect." That is the Lululemon philosophy. This means sweating and achieving fitness goals together, personal development through meditation, and being a community for like-minded people. Based on this, the vision of creating a place where people live up to this philosophy together was born.

Lululemon's strategy was to start offering fitness courses at its stores. Each week, employees move the furniture and products aside, roll out the yoga mats, and turn the stores into yoga studios. The courses are free of charge and are run by instructors from local studios of the community. Nowadays, this occurs at stores around the whole world. Customers come here to be inspired, and the stores become a meeting place with a great feel-good factor for like-minded people.

Thus, Lululemon became far more than just a place for purchasing products. With pleasant side effects. On the one hand, the stores are visited more frequently and the length of stay is extended, which also has a direct influence on sales. On the other hand, it allows employees to build closer relationships with their customers and understand their desires, goals, and passions.

Nowadays, the retailer is planning larger stores in order to create space for experience-related events. In Chicago, a store has been opened that has two exercise rooms, a meditation area, and a café. The store, which is 20,000 square feet in size, allows customers to train as if they were in a traditional yoga studio, with six to ten courses being offered every day. Should you forget your training outfit, you can borrow one from Lululemon without a problem and then get onto the mat.

In addition, a loyalty program has been developed in order to make the brand even more tangible for the fan community and to bring it even closer to Lululemon. Included in an annual fee of 128 dollars is a pair of pants or shorts at the same value. In addition, the program member can attend curated workout classes.

Lululemon plans and implements over 4000 events every year. The larger ones include, for example, the SeaWheeze half marathon in Vancouver or the ten-kilometer runs in Edmonton and Toronto. The smaller activities include free in-store meditation or yoga courses, running clubs, and other local events.

This is how Lululemon has become an authentic brand on the international market. Lululemon shows the world that it is not just a product but part of the community.

American Eagle Outfitters: Wash & Meet

American Eagle Outfitters, Inc. is an American lifestyle apparel and accessories chain with its headquarters in Pittsburgh, Pennsylvania. The company, which was founded in 1977, employs 40,000 workers and has more than 1200 stores worldwide. The stores, which average 5300 square feet in size, offer fashionable apparel, accessories, and care products to their target group of female and male students. The average age of their customers is between 15 and 25.

The American Eagle Outfitters store in Union Square, in the center of New York City, is located in the direct vicinity of the New York University dormitory. In other words, this store could hardly be any closer to its target group. What, then, could make more sense than creating a community gathering place precisely at this point for the students living in the neighborhood? The result is the AE Studio. It offers a complete brand experience and is perfectly matched to its young customers.

The novelty is a wall integrated into the store made up of washers and dryers that can be used by the students free of charge. Laundromats have developed into an integral part of large cities in recent years. The reason for this is that often, small, extremely expensive apartments in Manhattan only have limited or no space for washers. Many New York rental apartments even forbid hooking up a washer, as the pipes aren't always suitable to be used for this purpose. American Eagle Outfitters has thereby tailored its service offer in this store precisely to the needs of its customers on a tight budget.

This covers a huge target group within walking distance. But that isn't enough. There is a "Maker's Shop" where jeans can be customized. The creativity of the customers is almost unlimited. From a multitude of patches to various leather labels on the back of the pants, everyone can design their own unique jeans.

On the top floor is a lounge with a view of the park. The lounge serves as a co-working space or a meeting place for chilling, by which time the jeans are washed and dried. The community area has large tables, a bar area, a lot of seating, sockets, and free Wi-Fi.

Laundromats, lounge and working areas, and a station for individual product design are all more than just useful services. With these offers, American Eagle Outfitters has become an established meeting place for students around the corner.

Capital One: Community Banking

Capital One Financial Corporation is a bank holding corporation specializing in credit cards, consumer banking, and commercial banking. Since its foundation in the US state of Virginia in 1994, more than 900 branches have been opened in the USA, Canada, and Great Britain. Among these are currently around 30 bank cafés. Capital One is the eighth largest bank in the USA, employing almost 50,000 workers.

Image 4.1   Capital One. (Source: Capital One)

It doesn't look good for the traditional local banking business with branches. Many subsidiaries are closing for good, so that the number of bank branches has been declining for several years. There are many reasons for this, but convenient online banking plays an essential role. But not everyone wants to or is able to digitally complete their banking transactions, such as transfers. This part of the local clientele is literally left out in the rain.

Sure, bank employees are no longer as busy or needed as in the past. However, a lot of financial issues still require an expert and a personal conversation in private. After all, when it comes to sensitive subjects, not everyone trusts the online world. Therefore, Capital One decided to oppose the trend with a strategy of its own. Today, the financial institution demonstrates what progressive branches of the future can look like.

In the USA, Capital One has established financial transactions with cafés. These offer hot drinks, food, free Wi-Fi, and a lot of seating to allow you to have a drink or work on your laptop in peace. There are also free ATMs and special areas where you can get advice from experts, the financial coaches, on all financial matters. The coffee shop areas are supplied by Peet's Coffee. If you order a coffee as a Capital One customer, you get it at half price.

And how successful is the coffee bank in its day-to-day business? Well, it is used as a normal café at first. The open interior design, with exposed ceilings and various wooden structures, makes the cafés a popular community gathering place for working or relaxing, as it has community tables, chairs, couches, private corners, workspaces, conference rooms, interactive screens, and sockets everywhere.

In addition to free money coaching, there are events on financial planning, film evenings, or free yoga classes for the community. Here, you can just enjoy your coffee in a peaceful environment and, if you want to, inquire about financial products and concepts. A really important factor of this strategy is that there are no hard pressure sales teams or tactics forcing you into a discussion about banking products. The financial coaches only talk about finances, online banking, or Capital One if the conversation is initiated by the customer. This reserved form of interaction creates trust. It strengthens and expands the relationship with a loyal customer base.

With the Capital One cafés, the banking business becomes accessible to everyone again. At the same time, the brand can be experienced in a natural and relaxed way. The concept is geared entirely toward the needs of the target group. It creates customer relationships with an emotional bond. All this has been more than successful. With its community banking, Capital One has revolutionized the branch business.

Barclays: Local Leader in Innovation

Barclays PLC is a multinational financial service company specializing in retail and corporate banking and asset and investment management. Barclay PLC was founded in London in 1690 and has long been known for its innovations. In 1967, Barclays provided the world's first ATMs. Today, the company has more than 1300 branches in 50 countries, employing more than 82,000 workers.

In the past, banks played a central role in cities and communities. They were as indispensable in their social structure as part of the public sector as the church or the marketplace were. Digital development has also changed the social spaces of our society, places where more than just business is done. Where bank branches close, places of the local community disappear as well.

Against the background of this development, Barclays developed a concept that was supposed to make local branches relevant again in a new way. In these places, start-up companies and individuals were expected to find support for innovative projects.

Eagle Labs began in 2016 as an experiment with the overarching objective of enabling local businesses to participate in and drive the digital revolution. For this purpose, residents, customers, scientists, and companies from key industries were brought together. Together, start-ups and entrepreneurs were supposed to get help on site to realize their visions. Community rooms, resources, and expert knowledge were necessary for that to be achieved. Eagle Lab provided all this.

The great success of the first concept implementation was followed by expansion to other Barclays locations. A special area of expertise is tailored to the needs of local companies and the regional economic strength of the respective industries. It offers access to necessary resources such as expert mentoring, 3D printers, or laser cutters. Thus, prototypes of new products can be produced on site both quickly and cost-effectively.

In addition, each Eagle Lab offers an event room for workshops or boot camps to support local companies. School classes are invited in order to inspire the younger generation, making the Lab not just a place for companies but a place that makes new technologies accessible for everyone. After all, absolutely anyone can use these facilities.

The introduction of the Eagle Labs is not only tremendous support for companies in local communities. They are also an effective initiative for the success of an entire region. Thus, Barclays creates a sense of community while at the same time deepening its relationships with local entrepreneurs. Barclays emerges as a trustworthy brand.

Bibliography

American Eagle Outfitters. 2017. American Eagle Outfitters Unveils New Concept Store, AE Studio, in Union Square NYC. http://investors.ae.com/news-releases/news-releases-details/2017/American-Eagle-Outfitters-Unveils-New-Concept-Store-AE-Studio-in-Union-Square-NYC/default.aspx.

BankNews. Capital One 360 and Peet's Coffee & Tea Expand Relationship in 360 Cafés. https://www.banknews.com/blog/capital-one-360-and-peets-coffee-tea-expand-relationship-in-360-cafes/.

Barclays. 2019. Title. https://home.barclays/news/2019/8/second-scottish-eagle-lab-to-take-flight-in-aberdeen/.

Lululemon. History. https://info.lululemon.com/about/our-story/history.

———. Lululemon and Yoga. https://info.lululemon.com/about/our-story/lululemon-yoga.

Part II

Retail Technologies

In-store technologies are a big topic of discussion in the brick-and-mortar retail industry. Acronyms like VR, AR, AI, or RFID sound somewhat cryptic. Everyone has probably heard them before. But what exactly do they all mean, and what real benefit do these technologies offer the retail industry? Just to make one thing clear: The introduction of these technologies cannot be avoided. That's an established fact. After all, the opportunities they offer are downright overwhelming. Nonetheless, it seems that the majority of retailers are still holding back instead of utilizing the advantages of in-store technologies now to be one or, even better, several steps ahead of their competitors.

Technologies like augmented reality (AR) allow you to enhance the "reality of your store." This means going beyond the physical elements. Virtual reality (VR), on the other hand, creates a new reality. This allows further experiences to be created or pain points in the customer experience to be eliminated.

These are very obvious customer experiences, of course. However, in-store technologies have a lot to offer that isn't obvious, which is a good thing. The less a customer notices the technologies behind the experiences created, the better. Artificial intelligence (AI) can thus combine an infinite amount of information, evaluate it with algorithms, and add to it automatically, so that the applications are almost unlimited—from customer service with the entire corporate knowledge to predictions of upcoming collections to an analysis of someone's mood based on a customer's facial expression. Almost anything is possible.

RFID technology is just as fascinating. It works primarily in the background with radio frequency identification. It keeps inventories up to date in real time, retraces the paths customers take on the sales floor, and provides data on customer behavior.

So, what will it be? Customer experience, process optimization, time saving....? The question ultimately is: What are the right technologies for your company and its goals? We're about to get to the bottom of this.

5

Augmented Reality

Almost everyone was aware of the hype in 2016 surrounding the mobile phone game "Pokémon Go." People everywhere were running around the streets staring at their smartphones in order to find and catch the colorful Pokémon. According to the mobile phone display, it appeared as if the virtual creatures were directly there where the player was—like at the bus stop, on the shopping street, or behind the tree in the park. The app introduced the topic of augmented reality (AR) and its uses to the masses after it was downloaded more than a billion times.

Augmented reality refers to an enhancement of the actual reality through additional content with videos or similar items. The core of AR technology is the integration of digital information into the user's real environment. All you need to use it is a smartphone or tablet and the appropriate apps. Pictures or patterns are recognized via the mobile device's camera. They activate the software by giving the command, for example, to play a video or blend in information. Thus, the real environment is connected to the augmented reality.

The "Pokémon Go" phenomenon got players to leave their homes and search for virtual Pokémon out on the streets. What could this mean for retailers? Well, they can bring this type of customer experience to their stores, too. In addition to interactive entertainment possibilities, AR also offers a variety of options to eliminate obstacles or challenges during in-store visits and, at best, to convert them into a positive experience.

The more products are available to choose from, the more difficult it is to make a decision. We have all experienced this. If you want to try all the options

© The Author(s) 2020
M. Spanke, *Retail Isn't Dead*, https://doi.org/10.1007/978-3-030-36650-6_5

on top of that, the shopping experience can quickly become stressful. But not if you apply augmented reality. "Magic mirrors" allow customers to click through the collection and virtually see the goods on their own body. With just a click, lipsticks and eye shadows can virtually be tested on their own face, allowing the products to be tried without frustration or stress. It not only saves time but is fun as well.

One of the big advantages of online trading is the ease with which a product can be found. A physical store can't compete with this. At the same time, however, the virtual world offers help in the form of navigation technologies, for example. Apps with AR and motion tracking technology provide efficient directions and guide you to the desired products in real time like a GPS. This technology, too, is a time saver and real frustration killer.

Thus, augmented reality can be integrated into a marketing strategy in a creative and innovative way. Each experience can be customized and tailored exactly to fit each campaign. Seasonal adjustments are simply implemented at the touch of a button. Thus, you can change from one month to the next—from the summer campaign to the fall campaign, for example—provided the appropriate preparations have been made.

In order to survive in this digitally driven world, you need to be creative. Augmented reality can help you keep up with the competition or even be ahead of it. AR can also be applied on a small marketing budget, as the basic applications are affordable. The number of applications doesn't matter but rather the fact that with creativity, a weakness of the customer experience is turned into a positive brand event. However, it's important to develop such applications in a professional manner. After all, whoever offers the use of technologies needs to ensure that they result in a positive experience for the customer.

Call to Action

- Define which aspect of the customer journey can be improved through augmented reality.
- Consider what the concept of the AR experience can look like for this aspect of the customer journey.
- Don't just implement the technology for the sake of having it but rather for the purpose of offering customers real added value.

Charlotte Tilbury: Simulated Styling

Charlotte Tilbury is a British make-up artist and founder, Chairman, President and Chief Creative Officer of the makeup and skincare brand Charlotte Tilbury Beauty. The London company has eight stores in Los Angeles, London, Qatar, Dubai, Abu Dhabi, Kuwait and Hong Kong. In addition, the products are sold in multi-brand stores and e-commerce sites across United Kingdom, North America, Europe, the Middle East and Asia. Currently, almost 1000 people work for Charlotte Tilbury Beauty Ltd.

Image 5.1   Charlotte Tilbury. (Source: Charlotte Tilbury)

Charlotte Tilbury has worked as a make-up artist for many large brands, celebrities, and models. The results of her work decorate the title pages of top magazines like "Vogue" and "Vanity Fair." Shortly after introducing her beauty and skincare brand, it became a huge success. From the very beginning, Tilbury's products had a strong digital presence in beauty tutorials, and this attachment to new technologies is reflected at the stores. "Magic mirrors" with very sophisticated augmented reality technology are available there to the customers.

Customers can book a 45-minute makeover at the stores, for which they must choose one of ten typical Tilbury looks. Often, that isn't so easy, so special "magic mirrors" were developed to facilitate the decision-making process. The customer just sits in front of the mirror and chooses one of the looks, which is simulated realistically and in detail and adapted to the individual face. The customer's lips, eyes, and make-up are transformed in real time through augmented reality. All ten looks can also be presented next to each other at the same time and in less than a minute. It is easier to decide in comparison which look suits you best.

Customers can turn, blink their eyes, and see all the details up close. The chosen look authentically follows every movement. The entire product range can be virtually customized at the touch of a button. All looks can be saved for comparison or shared directly on social networks. There is also help for those who don't trust their subjective tastes: The mirrors have an artificial intelligence application that recommends a look to each customer based on an algorithm.

This augmented reality technology was developed through close collaboration with the make-up artists. This was the best way to understand how the products are supposed to be used and how they can be presented in the mirror realistically. No easy feat. It took several months to digitally match colors, shapes, skin tones, and facial recognition realistically.

Charlotte Tilbury's magic mirrors offer a lot of advantages. They help with the decision-making process, replace testers for sales support, and are a much more hygienic alternative to the classic method. In addition to commercial success, the mirror has also contributed to emotional success: It creates a connection between the customer and the brand in a playful manner.

Zara: Shop the Look

Zara SA is a Spanish fast-fashion retailer that belongs to one of the world's largest clothing retailer, the Inditex Group. The company, which was founded in 1975, has 2250 stores in almost 100 markets. It is known for its highly responsive supply chain. Once the products have been designed, they only need ten to fifteen days to get to the stores. With its selection of women's, men's, and children's clothing, the company is aimed at women and men who are very interested in the latest fashion trends.

Those who walked past a Zara shop window in 2018 were probably surprised to find a window without merchandise. All that could be seen was a sign in bold print saying, "Shop the Look in Augmented Reality," with brief instructions on how it works. After downloading the Zara app onto your smartphone, you aim the camera at the shop window, and a virtual fashion show begins to run on the mobile phone's display, with the shop window as the actual frame.

At more than 100 stores worldwide, customers were offered various augmented reality experiences for a limited time period. In addition to the aforementioned shop window, the smartphone app allowed podiums at the store or the dispatch boxes for online purchases to be animated. The in-store experiences featured holograms of models wearing exactly the outfits that were presented at the store. In seven to twelve-second sequences, the models posed and even spoke with the customers. Now you could click directly on "Shop the Look" and order the articles online or just grab them at the store. Customers were encouraged to take photos of the holograms and to share them on social networks through the app.

Think big: In order to achieve this augmented reality experience, a 1800 square feet stage was equipped with 68 cameras. The model sequences were created on the stage so that they could be brought to life virtually in the store at any time. For this purpose, the stores were equipped with Wi-Fi networks.

Zara has shown impressively how AR technology can be utilized in brick-and-mortar retail in an unusual way. Customers are interactively involved and can experience the glamour of a fashion show almost live.

Bibliography

Charlotte Tilbury. The Magic Mirror in Store. https://www.charlottetilbury.com/uk/blog/2018/05/charlotte-tilbury-magic-mirror/.

Sandler, Emma. 2018. Zara Stores Target Millennials with Augmented Reality Displays. *Forbes*. https://www.forbes.com/sites/emmasandler/2018/04/16/zara-stores-targets-millennials-with-augmented-reality-displays/#79b7b2692315.

Schygulla, Julia. 2018. Zara startet mit Augmented Reality. https://www.textilwirtschaft.de/business/news/e-commerce-zara-startet-mit-augmented-reality-209623.

Street, Chloe. 2018. Zara to Launch an Augmented Reality App in Its Stores. *Evening Standard*. https://www.standard.co.uk/fashion/zara-to-launch-an-augmented-reality-app-in-its-stores-a3789441.html.

6

Virtual Reality

Flying to the moon in a rocket, experiencing weightlessness, and jumping around on the surface of the moon like the astronaut Neil Armstrong did in Apollo 11 is a dream, at least for many youngsters. Adults maybe dream a bit smaller, of paragliding at 12,000 feet over glaciers and snow-covered mountains, for example… Whatever happens to be on your personal bucket list, some of it you'll probably not be able to realize. However, virtual reality lets almost any dream come true. With VR, we can go anywhere and be part of anything, at least virtually.

Virtual reality is an artificially created reality in which users can move around. In contrast to augmented reality, the real environment is not included here. Instead, VR can create the real world virtually along with any other environment. Here, the same technology is used as for video games. Objects can be inserted anywhere as 3D models and, following the appropriate programming, be utilized by the user in an interactive way. It is also possible to use real film data that have been recorded with 360-degree cameras. However, the user's interaction is very limited in this case. In contrast to AR, VR cannot readily be implemented on a smartphone. This is because in addition to VR glasses, you also need to use input devices if you want to utilize the artificial space in an interactive way.

VR offers a lot of opportunities for the brick-and-mortar retail business. The technology can create an additional in-store experience for customers. With VR, for example, they sit in the front row of a New York Fashion Week show. Here, the models naturally present products offered by the company. VR is nothing less than a revolution in experience marketing. The connection between customers and a brand is established by offering an entertaining and maybe even unique experience.

© The Author(s) 2020
M. Spanke, *Retail Isn't Dead*, https://doi.org/10.1007/978-3-030-36650-6_6

Product tutorials in the form of instructional videos on using the products offered can also be implemented in an exciting way with virtual reality. Thus, customers can be better informed, or employees can be trained more effectively thanks to virtual experiences.

Some products cannot readily be tested at the store or at least not in the real environment. From this point of view, too, VR can be applied in many different ways. The technology can, for example, offer a view of how furniture in the entire room looks or a test drive in a self-configured car model. It's easier for customers to picture a product as part of their lives if they see it in a seemingly real environment. That way, the desired product can be tested virtually to facilitate the decision-making process. Closely linking exciting experiences to the products being sold makes it possible to effectively appeal to customers on an emotional level.

Returns are an integral part of retailing. Today, in the brick-and-mortar business, they constitute around ten percent. In online trading, they are about twice to three times as high. This is where VR comes into play. The number of returns was demonstrably reduced if products could be tested by the customer in a virtual reality experience.

A further advantage of VR lies in the fact that the sales area can be virtually enlarged and the real inventory reduced. Let's take the furniture industry as an example. A large selection means that a large display area is required as well. With VR, this can be adjusted by an unlimited number of feet, without the high costs of renting space. At the same time, there's no need for all products to be available on site. Potential customers can be inspired with an entire furniture line without having to present the real products as samples. This entails great savings potential for production and display samples and logistics, storage, and rental costs.

Virtual reality applications can also provide information about customer behavior by making it possible to track physical reactions—for example, how the customer interacts with the products in the virtual environment. This advanced knowledge offers a great opportunity for retailers. Exactly as with AR systems, changing to a new collection or season can happen at the touch of a button. Everything can be adjusted in advance and changed at the stores from one day to the next with little effort.

A VR experience is thus almost perfect for customer retention. The entertaining interaction with the brand turns it into an experience. However, the application needs to be well thought out and specific in terms of the target group. The customers' needs and wishes have to be addressed. After all, the focus is on the target group and not on the technology.

Call to Action

- Define the possible added value of virtual reality at the point of sale from the customers' perspective.
- Make sure that the value is easy for the customer to understand and the technology is intuitive to use.
- Remember that it should be fun to use virtual reality.

The North Face: Desert Expedition in the Big City

The North Face was founded in San Francisco, USA in 1966 as a retail store for climbing equipment. Since 2000, the company has belonged to VF Cooperation and has its headquarters in Alameda, California. The outdoor brand for high-performance apparel, shoes, equipment, and accessories employs around 1000 workers, and the products are sold around the world at 3500 locations. The target group involves women and men between the ages of 18 and 34, with the focus being on men.

Image 6.1 The North Face. (Source: The North Face)

The North Face's mission is to awaken people's interest in nature and to take them on one of their numerous expeditions. But how do you inspire customers at an urban mall? The North Face has asked itself this question. Its response is to invite its customers on virtual expeditions to two American cult sites. The first one is the beautiful Yosemite National Park in the Sierra Nevada mountains of California. The second one is the Moab desert in Utah, which boasts massive red rock formations. In order to have as many customers as possible participate in the expeditions, breath-taking virtual reality experiences were created.

The VR experience allows customers to test equipment at the store and be sent on a tour with The North Face athletes Cedar Wright and Sam Elias. The viewers feel as if they are there live when the two prepare a rope, climb, and make their plans for the next day. If the customer puts on the headset, he or she is in the middle of the action, completely free to look around in any direction and experience every moment of the adventure as if he or she were actually there.

The fact that the VR experience is so convincing is due to the high-quality material with which it was programmed. A group of athletes and filmmakers worked together with The North Face on site to produce the content. Everything was recorded with 360-degree cameras, stereoscopic 3D cameras, and advanced 3D sound field microphones.

Virtual reality allows The North Face to tell its stories so convincingly that viewers enjoy immersing themselves in this world and testing the equipment that way. This experience creates a close connection to the topic and thus to the brand. People prefer to buy from companies with which they have an emotional bond.

Lowe's: Award-Winning "Holoroom"

Lowe's Companies, Inc. is a FORTUNE® 50 home improvement company serving more than 18 million customers a week in the United States and Canada. Lowe's and its related businesses operate or service more than 2200 home improvement and hardware stores and employ approximately 300,000 associates.

Research shows many DIY projects don't get started because customers don't have the confidence to complete their projects independently. For this reason, Lowe's Innovation Labs has developed several prototypes that use virtual reality to give customers 'hands-on' experience with home improvement projects and tools. These prototypes are comprehensive, multi-sensory virtual reality experiences that combine visual elements, haptics and sound to create an immersive virtual experience.

In "Holoroom How To," Lowe's customers can learn basic DIY skills. They learn everything about the material required and the steps for completion, all in an entertaining, interactive virtual reality environment. For example, one program teaches customers how to tile a shower. This new type of training gives customers the knowledge and confidence to implement their projects independently.

Lowe's Innovation Labs also created a concept that satisfies customers' need to "try before you buy" in an innovative way. In "Holoroom Test Drive," customers can try a power tool, like a hedge trimmer, in a virtual garage and backyard environment. To make the experience as realistic as possible, there is a customized control system with a lifelike weight, with which the customer develops a feel for using the tool. Customers can not only try new products, they receive tips from professionals in order to facilitate the decision-making process.

This concept has been implemented successfully in several stores and received the Auggie Award at the Augmented World Expo 2018 for the best business solution.

IKEA: Moving Furniture Virtually

IKEA is the world's largest furniture dealer and was founded in Sweden in 1943 by Ingvar Kamprad, who at the time was 17 years old. Today, the company employs around 211,000 workers. IKEA designs and sells ready-to-assemble furniture, kitchen appliances, and household products at over 400 stores in more than 50 countries.

Image 6.2   IKEA. (Source: Demodern—Creative Technologies)

When purchasing furniture, you can measure it to see if it will fit into a room, but not everyone can imagine how the furniture will actually look in that room in the end. For this purpose, the virtual reality experience "IKEA Immerse" was developed by the digital agency Demodern. And there's more: Not only is the room virtually furnished with this VR application, but customers can even interact with the furniture, moving it through the rooms and placing it as desired. This customer experience is currently available at select stores in Germany.

Customers are able to individually furnish a virtual living room or kitchen from hundreds of options and configuration possibilities. Equipped with headsets, the users are guided through the application by the brand testimonials named Jonas and Smilla via voice-over. The intuitive user surface and interaction design makes it possible for customers of any age to use the application.

The intention with the virtual reality experience was to create an environment that felt real and was vivid. The wood, metal, and glass textures look real, and the materials change in texture and brightness depending on the light penetration and time of day. If you listen carefully, you will also notice the sound of the products and habitation noise, as they were recorded in real places and at an IKEA store. These are noises from home and outside, for example, children playing or cars driving by. When you enter the kitchen, the narrator tells you about his favorite dish.

This VR experience also allows interaction between different users. Social media was considered as well: A panoramic image of the room can be shared directly on social networks. In addition, a mobile shopping list can be created directly from all articles in the configured room.

Customers love the "IKEA Immerse" experience, so it has established itself as an in-store VR experience. After all, the virtual room beckons you to try out, configure, share, and come back again.

Audi: A 3D Simulator Leading to Your Dream Car

Audi AG is a German carmaker of premium vehicles that belongs to the Volkswagen Group. It was founded in 1899 and has its headquarters in Ingolstadt. The company employs over 90,000 workers worldwide, 60,000 of which at the German sites in Ingolstadt and Neckarsulm. The car manufacturer is active in more than 100 markets and is continuously growing.

Image 6.3 Audi. (Source: AUDI AG)

Purchasing a new vehicle is a big investment. Customers who spend that much money on a vehicle want to define as many details as possible. In the past, consumers used brochures to customize their car and then had to hope that in reality, everything would look as they had imagined in their mind's eye. Audi has solved this flaw in the car purchase and turned that into an exciting shopping experience.

The "Customer Private Lounge" is currently available at over 400 Audi dealers worldwide. It consists of a comfortable sitting area with an optional virtual reality headset and a 75-inch screen. On this screen, a sales consultant presents the entire Audi product range with all the colors, features, and configuration options. Then it's your turn. The customer can configure the car according to his or her own taste and individual needs.

Once everything has been assembled, the individually created car can be experienced virtually in three dimensions and 360-degree mode in full size. The future owner can see the colors and configurations during the drive as well and interact with the vehicle. For example, the doors can be opened and closed or the headlights turned on and off, all under different lighting conditions at different times of the day with the associated sound effects.

This VR experience configures the cars down to the smallest detail and allows the interior of the vehicle to be viewed close up and from every angle. Through the use of high-fidelity 4K rendering, a realistic appearance is created. All VR visualizations were created based on the entire development and construction process of the vehicles. The basis involves the visualizations of the master vehicle models, which contain every single plate, every screw, and every conceivable fastening element.

The "Customer Private Lounge" has become a valuable sales tool for Audi. It offers customers detailed information and maximum security as they make a purchase decision.

Bibliography

Audi. 2017. Audi Launches Virtual Reality Technology in Dealerships. https://www.audi-mediacenter.com/en/press-releases/audi-launches-virtual-reality-technology-in-dealerships-9270.

Demodern. IKEA Immerse. https://demodern.com/projects/ikea-vr-immerse.

Jaunt XR. 2018. The North Face and Jaunt Create and Launch "The North Face VR" Leading With Breathtaking Virtual Reality Experiences in Yosemite National Park and Moab. https://www.jauntxr.com/news/the-north-face-and-jaunt/.

Lowe's Innovation Labs. Holoroom How To. http://www.lowesinnovationlabs.com/holoroomhowto.

———. Holoroom Test Drive. http://www.lowesinnovationlabs.com/testdrive.

7

Artificial Intelligence

People everywhere talk about the countless applications of artificial intelligence, AI, in the retail business. But what exactly is that in the first place? Artificial intelligence is a branch of computer science. It simulates human intelligence by solving problems, receiving and issuing commands, and automating tasks for people. It is based on algorithms that are capable of learning from experiences. This actually sounds quite intelligent. The benefit is that tasks are implemented more efficiently, accurately, and cost-effectively than by people, which in turn may sound somewhat threatening. Examples for the use of AI include understanding human speech or autonomously driving a car.

Artificial intelligence is increasingly finding its way into commerce, but not in ways we might imagine. Even in the future, we probably won't always be surrounded by robots driving around. AI will barely be visible to customers and yet have a big impact on business operations and the customer experience, for example, with applications for sales and customer relationship management (CRM) or personalized consumer recommendations. The use of AI will increasingly affect areas in commerce such as manufacturing, logistics, and delivery as well as payment processing and services.

Warehousing can be optimized with this trendsetting technology in order to improve the customer experience. Artificial intelligence, for example, helps customers find the desired product, informs employees when something needs to be restocked, or calculates the optimal balance of product quantity, storage space use, anticipated demand, and profit. AI can likewise be used for pricing. We are already used to prices constantly fluctuating for gasoline at gas stations or for flights and hotels—today, AI generally is behind this as well. Thus, for example, Amazon.com adjusts its prices with AI several million

M. Spanke, *Retail Isn't Dead*, https://doi.org/10.1007/978-3-030-36650-6_7

times a day, based on data information on trends, the season, availability, demand, or even competitor prices.

Artificial intelligence in customer service can significantly improve the quality of service, as customer problems or inquiries are answered in real time. Information can be customized based on location, season, or other criteria that vary from store to store. AI, for example, makes recommendations for products that are available at the respective store. Conversely, it can also avoid suggestions for products that are already out of stock or otherwise unavailable at that location. Some technologies scan faces during use in order to identify and respond to dissatisfied customers. Thus, for example, the system recognizes an agitated consumer and sends a sales employee immediately to offer assistance. In addition, customer wait times can be shortened, and business operating costs can be reduced through staff reductions.

Probably the best shopping experience is achieved if customer expectations are recognized in advance. Fortunately, thoughts can't be read before the customer expresses them in words, but almost: Facial recognition provides demographic information like age, gender, and ethnic heritage. This enables AI systems to display personalized product recommendations. There are also in-store systems that are linked to smartphone apps and inform the store team which customer has just entered the shop and how his or her previous purchasing behavior was. As "transparent" as we may feel here, it means an enormous information advantage for any sales conversation. If a customer is greeted by name and recommended suitable products right away, the shopping experience will be near perfect.

Artificial intelligence can play an important role in the location-related planning of promotional calendars. With the data from previous promotions on products, customer frequency, preferences, sales figures, etc., AI can create a promotional calendar based on the buying behavior at the respective store.

The applications of artificial intelligence in retail are endless, but brick-and-mortar businesses are still not taking advantage of the potential. The biggest challenge is the collection of data at the physical store. Online providers have the advantage of having a wealth of data information on customer behavior. From navigation through the product range to product preferences, prices, regional differences, and much more information. In brick-and-mortar retail, there may be data on transactions and customer cards, but this isn't sufficient for machine learning. To comprehensively use the possibilities offered by AI, complex systems are needed that are usually quite expensive. But the investment is worth it to optimize internal processes and offer customers a unique service and thus a unique brand experience.

Call to Action

- Define weaknesses in the business processes and in the customers' purchasing process.
- Ask yourself with which information you can remove these weaknesses.
- Get expert advice on which systems can be used to generate and provide the desired information in order to eliminate the weaknesses.

HSBC: Meet Pepper

HSBC is a multinational bank and financial services holding that was founded in Hong Kong in 1865. The four global business areas include retail banking and wealth management, commercial banking, global banking and markets, and global private banking. HSBC is one of the largest banking and financial services organizations worldwide with more than 240,000 employees and branches in 65 countries in Europe, Asia, the Middle East and Africa, North America and Latin America.

Image 7.1   HSBC. (Source: BIG IDEAS Visual Merchandising Inc)

HSBC wants to become the "Bank of the Future" in retail banking. Appropriate steps have been taken by the bank in order to realize this vision. The biggest change for customers is the introduction of Pepper, the engaging, social humanoid robot, to HSBC's bank branches. Not only is the little fellow extremely helpful, but it also looks really cute with its big eyes.

Pepper is a humanoid robot with a tablet attached to its chest that can move independently on wheels. Pepper has arms and hands so that a handshake is possible as well. After all, Pepper is a robot for people. It is full of knowledge and offers customers basic product information and options for self-service banking with its integrated interactive screen.

Upon entering the HSBC branch, customers are greeted by Pepper in a friendly manner, and their needs are identified with a few questions. In the course of the conversation, the robot collects data on the customers' preferences, characteristics, and habits in order to personalize its answers accordingly. Since Pepper is very much like a colleague, if prompted it can pass along information to bank employees, which allows the team to focus on the essential points during its conversation with the customers. The robot unites the digital world with the real one and supports the staff. Don't worry, Pepper has no intention of replacing its colleagues. It just makes processes more effective by completing routine tasks. This saves time, which benefits everyone involved. By the way, Pepper does not have access to customer data or personal banking information.

The robot communicates with words, eyes, and body language, and customers have a lot of fun interacting with it. Pepper is memorable, informative, always friendly, positive, and professional. With it, visiting the bank becomes an unforgettable and extraordinary experience. No wonder Pepper has been the star among robots on social networks since its introduction. With a campaign, HSBC asked its customers to take photos with Pepper and to share them. The hashtags are #MeetPepper and #PoseWithPepper.

HSBC was the first financial institution in the USA to introduce robot technology for private banking. Since then, transaction volumes at ATMs and new credit card applications have increased. In the New York branch alone, year over year business grew by 60 percent.

Amazon Books: The Algorithm of Our Desires

Amazon is the world's largest e-commerce company and has its headquarters in the US state of Washington. It was founded in 1994 and currently employs around 650,000 workers. In 2015, Amazon Books was opened in Seattle, Washington as the company's first physical bookstore. Today, there are around 20 of these shops. The stores, which are on average 4000 to 10,000 square feet in size, carry books, tablets, and smart home devices.

Image 7.2   Amazon Books. (Source: BIG IDEAS Visual Merchandising Inc)

Consumers rely on good advice when making purchase decisions—advice from friends, family, or product reviews. Customers wanting purchase advice are being guided more and more by artificial intelligence. Data-based knowledge allows retailers to immerse themselves more in customization and thus to develop solutions to recommend customers the best and most suitable products. Who knows which book on a particular subject has received the best reviews? Amazon.com does and thus Amazon Books as well.

There is a wealth of data available to the online giant, which is the basis for the fundamental concept of Amazon Books. A sophisticated system is used to bring the best-selling and most popular books into the physical stores. Amazon offers customers exactly what they currently want according to these data.

Even the way the inventory is selected and sorted is based on customer data with a human touch. All articles in the store are rated with four or more stars, or are top sellers, or are new and trending at Amazon.com. The aisles are categorized by section as you would expect them to be at a bookstore: fiction, children, young adults, cooking, biographies, etc. There are also Amazon-specific areas with book titles that are set up using the Amazon data collected. "If you like…You'll love…" or "Most-Wished-For Books on Amazon.com."

Sure, these bookshops only carry a relatively low number of books. They also don't have the required volume of specific stock. But they are well equipped and very innovative. Every title has a card with the Amazon star rating and an excerpt of the customer reviews. Digital price tags alongside every product in store enable customers to see not only the price and Prime price, but also their Prime Member savings, the average star rating, and the number of reviews a product has received. In addition, there are price scanners located throughout the entire store. At the shop, Amazon Prime members pay the online price for books, while non-Prime customers pay the list price, which is higher at times.

As an extension of Amazon.com, Amazon Books is an absolutely logical consequence. Thanks to artificial intelligence, customers here are presented exactly what most of them are looking for now or what is sure to suit their wishes. After all, Amazon's AI recognizes customers' desires sooner than the customers themselves.

Uniqlo: "Neuro-Headset" for the Purchase Decision

Uniqlo Co. Ltd. was founded in Japan in 1949. It is a subsidiary of Fast Retailing Co. Ltd., runs close to 2200 stores worldwide, and employs over 44,000 workers. The stores are around 17,000 square feet in size and high-quality, innovative apparel that is universal in design and comfort.

Image 7.3   Uniqlo. (Source: Uniqlo)

If the selection is too large, we sometimes wish someone else would make the decision for us. Someone who knows exactly what we are looking for. Uniqlo set itself precisely this task. When there are over 600 different T-shirt designs available, it's only natural that customers are sometimes overwhelmed when it comes to deciding which T-shirt suits their individual and thus unique personality. UMood is the solution to the dilemma. It is artificial intelligence to indicate which apparel suits any single person's mood.

But what exactly is behind UMood? Select Uniqlo stores had UMood kiosks with AI technology for a limited period of time. Customers were equipped with a neuro-headset to measure their brain waves. While the user was shown different media like images and videos, neurological reactions occurred unbeknownst to him or her. Brain activity was then measured in terms of interest, stress, concentration, and sleepiness. These data were evaluated in real time by an algorithm customized for Uniqlo. Once the customer's current mood had been analyzed, the algorithm selected a series of matching Uniqlo T-shirts.

This experience may not be suitable for everyday life and surely doesn't offer permanent support for purchase decisions. But with this in-store technology, Uniqlo offered its customers a very personal and new experience: a "stylist" based on neuroscience and artificial intelligence.

H&M: Trend Scouts AI & Big Data

Hennes & Mauritz AB is a Swedish chain store that offers fast-fashion apparel for women, men, young people, and children. The retailer was founded in Stockholm in 1947, where the headquarters are still located today. With over 170,000 employees and almost 4500 branches in more than 60 countries, H&M is the second largest clothing retailer in the world. The company's core target group involves fashionable and trendy consumers.

Image 7.4   H&M. (Source: H&M)

Like many other companies, H&M has also had to struggle with strong profit declines. To change that, large investments were made in artificial intelligence. It was supposed to help create more efficient supply chains, optimize inventory levels and merchandise management, and predict trends better. The investments in the technology paid off: In just one year, H&M was able to achieve an enormous profit increase.

Just like other fast-fashion retailers, H&M is under enormous pressure to anticipate trends as early as possible. Since prices are affordable and profit margins small, collections that do not sell immediately pose a serious challenge. The unwanted stock has to be moved, and this causes additional costs. If the goods don't sell elsewhere, either, they have to be reduced, in which case the corresponding costs reduce the profit margin. Today, H&M uses large amounts of data and AI to predict fashion trends and preferences. A great help that allows the risk of hard-to-sell collections to be reduced.

In the past, all stores had more or less the same merchandise in their assortment, which led to frequent and above all national reductions of unsold inventory at many, many stores. Today, H&M solves this problem by tailoring supply and demand exactly to local customers. For this purpose, AI system algorithms analyze information from purchases, returns, and customer card data. This allows the respective inventory to be adapted to local customer needs. The result is that the right goods are assigned to the right stores on the right markets.

Investing in artificial intelligence was certainly the right step to take for the company. Data and AI algorithms are now used to predict trends more reliably, make merchandising decisions, and optimize supply chains and processes. Even if most of these steps are not really visible to the customer, they nevertheless contribute to a positive shopping experience because what people want is available on site in an optimal amount.

Bibliography

Isobar. A Neurological Shopping Experience. https://www.isobar.com/global/en/work/uniqlo-umood/

Marr, Bernard. 2018. How Fashion Retailer H&M Is Betting on Artificial Intelligence and Big Data to Regain Profitability. *Forbes*. https://www.forbes.com/sites/bernardmarr/2018/08/10/how-fashion-retailer-hm-is-betting-on-artificial-intelligence-and-big-data-to-regain-profitability/#4e1c54135b00.

McCarthy, Tom. 2017. Amazon's First New York Bookstore Blends Tradition with Technology. *The Guardian*. https://www.theguardian.com/technology/2017/may/26/amazon-new-york-bookstore.

Price, Emily. 2018. Pepper the Robot Has a New Job at HSBC Bank. *Fortune*. https://fortune.com/2018/06/27/pepper-the-robot-hsbc-job/.

Uniqlo. UMood. https://www.uniqlo.com/au/store/umood.

8

RFID: Radio Frequency Identification

What does good old radio have to do with new smart technology that's bringing retail up to speed? Well, radio waves perfectly come in handy in this industry with so-called radio frequency identification. With RFID, radio waves are used to collect data from small chips called tags. In practice, this means that a reading device is used that interprets and transmits radio signals. If a tag is nearby, it receives the signal and sends a message back to the reading device, which identifies the tag and receives the data contained on it. Reading devices can be hand scanners, door scanners, and even mobile phones. Tags are small chips that can be embedded into objects like smart cards, key rings, and stickers.

When used in brick-and-mortar retail, it very quickly allows you to gain an exact overview of inventory. Counting products or manually scanning each article when taking inventory is very time-consuming, and staff deployment is cost-intensive. RFID scanners can read tags from a distance of up to 20 feet and capture hundreds of tags per second. Permanently installed RFID scanners provide real-time monitoring of inventory levels. Their use makes it a lot easier to always have a sufficient quantity of products available to customers.

With this technology, it is possible to accurately track if and where the products are being moved. When a supermarket integrates RFID tags into its shopping carts, this gives an overview anytime of when they left the store or even the premises and when they were returned. Thus, tags can also provide information on whether there are currently enough shopping carts for customers in the parking lot. The same function can be used as protection against theft. Comparing payment information with the individual article ID can trigger a theft alarm as soon as an unpaid article passes an exit reader.

© The Author(s) 2020
M. Spanke, *Retail Isn't Dead*, https://doi.org/10.1007/978-3-030-36650-6_8

In addition, RFID enables an automated payment process. Customers can scan articles with an app on their mobile phone and automatically pay with payment systems like Google Pay or Apple Pay. Alternatively, all articles can be simultaneously scanned and paid for by card while passing through the checkout line. This makes shopping very customer-friendly and saves consumers a lot of time.

RFID also offers new possibilities when it comes to marketing. Tags on in-store POS advertising materials can contain helpful data for customers. Mobile phones can be used to retrieve information through an appropriately programmed app. That could include, for example, detailed product specifications, availability, or a discount coupon that can be redeemed right at the store.

When customers pay with credit, debit, or customer discount cards, the purchases can be linked to the RFID data collected. That way, all customer movements can be accurately tracked, making it easier to understand customer behavior in order to make appropriate improvements. This knowledge can be used, for example, to optimize the store layout, modify the paths customers take, or place individual products into better positions.

Today, it is relatively inexpensive to implement RFID. However, it only works if dealers and manufacturers cooperate and products already have an RFID tag or have one added retroactively. If that is the case, this technology offers retailers a lot of new possibilities and customers a better shopping experience.

Call to Action

- Consider if there are any pain points in your processes that can be corrected with RFID.
- Make sure that all articles from your retailers and manufacturers have RFID codes, or find a suitable alternative to attach the tags to your products.
- Define in advance which of the versatile functions of this technology you want to use and how it can be integrated into daily processes.

Pepe Jeans: Pants in Radio Communication

The denim brand Pepe Jeans was founded on Portobello Road in London in 1973 and now has its headquarters in Madrid in Spain. The company employs almost 2300 workers in over 500 stores and is represented in 54 countries. In addition to denim and street wear, the product range also includes accessories and shoes. The brand targets women and men between the ages of 18 and 40 as well as children and young people between the ages of four and 16.

Image 8.1   Pepe Jeans. (Source: Pepe Jeans)

Not everyone loves shopping. Especially if the search for new clothes looks like this: In the fitting room, the customer discovers that the pants he or she selected aren't the perfect size or don't have the perfect wash look. Now he or she needs to get dressed again and leave the fitting room to look for a new size or a different wash look. Once back in the fitting room, the little changing game starts all over again. How tedious. That's why customers generally only go into the fitting room once and only change clothes once. Whatever doesn't fit stays at the store.

At the London flagship store of Pepe Jeans, things are different. The fitting rooms are equipped with RFID technology and interactive screens. If a customer hangs up the articles he or she has just tried on in the fitting room, the RFID reader recognizes the radio signals of the tags on the clothes and the information stored. The products, sizes, colors, and styles of the respective articles are immediately displayed on a large screen on the opposite wall.

If, for example, the fit or color isn't perfect, a choice can be made right from the alternatives available at the store using the interactive screen. The system informs the sales staff, who immediately brings the articles to the fitting room. Thus, the customer can try the merchandise on right away, without the annoying clothes-on-clothes-off procedure and without having to leave the fitting room. This really is an innovative service that promises a positive customer experience. Pants with radio waves, a dream.

Lululemon: Yoga Meets Technology

Founded in 1998, Lululemon Athletica Inc. is a Canadian sportswear retailer. The company has its head office in Vancouver and has over 400 stores in North America, Asia, Europe, and Oceania. More than 13,000 employees work for the yoga-inspired company. Performance shirts, shorts, pants, as well as lifestyle apparel and yoga accessories for women and men are offered at the stores.

Just a few years ago, Lululemon used to experience a surplus of goods in its warehouses and a shortage of goods on the sales floors every now and then. This represented a serious problem in the customer experience if the desired merchandise or right size wasn't available at the store. The use of RFID technology almost completely solved this problem. The system has increased the inventory accuracy at the stores and warehouses to an impressive 98 percent.

The introduction happened within a short period of time. First, the RFID tags were printed and coded at more than 30 factories in 15 countries. Products without tags were reworked at the distribution center so that absolutely all articles would have a tag when they arrived at the stores. Within a period of just six months, the roll-out occurred at the 300 American stores.

Today, the RFID tags are read for the first time upon receipt of the goods at the stores. As soon as an article is moved from its respective storage area to the sales floor, its status is updated. In addition, the store teams count the inventory on a weekly basis, which only takes about half an hour thanks to the RFID technology.

In the past, two employees were required to replenish stock. They communicated with each other via walkie talkies to ensure that all products were available to customers on the sales floor. This really was "old school." Today, thanks to RFID technology, an exact overview of missing products is always available, and the corresponding tasks can now be completed throughout the day. In daily interaction with customers, all employees are equipped with handheld devices and an app so that they can check inventory at any time.

This has allowed store processes to be optimized and work hours to be reduced. All employees now have a real-time overview of inventory and know exactly where each article is currently available in which size. In addition, the app's RFID database shows online customers a nearby store where the selected product is available in the desired quantity, size, and color. This is the only way to make "Buy Online, Pickup in Store" possible in the first place.

By introducing RFID systems, Lululemon has managed not only to optimize its processes and improve the customer experience but also to increase revenue across all channels. The yogis and yoginis have put on a top performance there!

Macy's: Never "Out of Stock"

The American department store chain Macy's was founded by Roland Hussey Macy in New York in 1858. Since 2015, it has been the largest department store chain in the USA in terms of retail sales. With 1,250,000 square feet of sales space, the New York flagship store is even one of the largest department stores in the world. Around 130,000 workers are employed at the company's headquarters and the approximately 640 branches in the USA, Puerto Rico, and Guam, 38 Bloomingdale's stores and nearly 170 Bluemercury locations. The product range includes fashion, accessories, jewelry, cosmetics, fragrances, kitchen utensils, and furnishings. Macy's stores offer something for the whole family, but the main target group involves middle-class women between the ages of 16 and 34.

Image 8.2 Macy's. (Source: Macy's)

It is not uncommon for an article to be forgotten somewhere in stock, which means that the opportunity of selling it at the regular price is missed. As if that wasn't infuriating enough, a challenge from the digital side may be added—the article is advertised as available online through "Buy Online, Pickup in Store." In this case, not only do you lose revenue, but you also upset the customer. Macy's has solved this problem by equipping all articles at all stores with RFID tags. That way, you always know exactly where each product is located.

As early as several years ago, Macy's started to use and optimize RFID technology for its own purposes. Today, merchandise tracking is automated along the entire retail supply chain, from the warehouse to the store. The tags replace the tedious process of employees manually scanning products. RFID is not a current project at Macy's but already firmly integrated into business processes. And this is reflected in the results. Inventory accuracy has drastically improved, which means the number of out-of-stock articles has been massively reduced. The result: improved processes, sales, profit, and happier customers.

Bibliography

Gonzalez, Melissa. 2018. Innovative Use Cases Leveraging RFID in Retail. *Retail Touch Points*. https://www.retailtouchpoints.com/features/executive-viewpoints/innovative-use-cases-leveraging-rfid-in-retail.

Hendriksz, Vivian. 2017. Q&A: Pepe Jeans New Store Concept. FashionUnited. https://fashionunited.uk/news/fashion/q-a-pepe-jeans-new-store-concept/2017072425283.

NXP. NXP Ucode Helps Lululemon's Retail Outlets Stay Fit. https://www.nxp.com/docs/en/supporting-information/Lululemon-RFID-Success-Story.pdf.

Thau, Barbara. 2017. Is The 'RFID Retail Revolution' Finally Here? A Macy's Case Study. *Forbes*. https://www.forbes.com/sites/barbarathau/2017/05/15/is-the-rfid-retail-revolution-finally-here-a-macys-case-study/#7da992803294.

Part III

Inspired by Online Retail

It is no secret that e-commerce has fundamentally changed people's shopping habits. Customers expect a direct insight into available stock, a rapid product search, reviews from other consumers, and much more. These high standards put a lot of pressure on brick-and-mortar retail. The shift in customer behavior makes it essential for companies to make changes in order to keep up with this rising competitive pressure. Time and again, new challenges emerge. After all, in our globalized, digitized world, there no longer are any rest phases between essential developments and market innovations. Thus, change is the only constant in retail as well.

Online and offline shopping both have their particular advantages. At the store, customers can touch the products, test them, and take them home right away. The online shop can locate products for each customer within seconds, check the availability, make personalized offers, and much more. But who says that this isn't possible in physical retail as well? This chapter shows how the advantages of e-commerce can be transferred to physical stores, for the potential here is far from exhausted.

The beginning of this chapter is dedicated to social media that each store can and should use to its advantage. That can happen on portals from Facebook to Instagram to Pinterest or simply by designing the store in such a way that it becomes a popular motif for social media and customers grab their smartphones to take photos. Speaking of smartphones, do not underestimate company apps. With the right features, the software can do incredible things for customers at the store. These range from details on stock availability, product information, and personalized offers to the mobile in-store navigation device that directs the customer straight to the desired product.

The convenient payment methods for products at online shops can also be transferred to the physical retail store. Here, too, there are a variety of options for achieving this. Time is the decisive factor, as customers want a rapid process. This also applies to the provision of goods—whether for pickup or for home delivery. Returns are an annoying topic both online and offline. The digital customer has to repack the merchandise and mail it back. The consumer at the physical store has to take the time and effort to go back to the store while generally being prepared for wait times at the exchange counter. But there are solutions for this as well.

E-commerce has shown brick-and-mortar retail how it works. Now it's up to the physical retail market to use its new opportunities by adapting online solutions to its advantage and combining them with its own advantages. For customers, this represents the opportunity to get the best of both worlds in brick-and-mortar retail.

9

Social Networks

It may be somewhat clichéd to claim that millennials are incapable of eating a meal now without posting a photo of it. True to the motto—whatever wasn't posted on social media hasn't been experienced. As exaggerated as it may be, it has a kernel of truth to it. Facebook alone has over two billion users worldwide, two-thirds of which use the platform on a daily basis. This network, along with others, thus becomes the key component of the brand strategy of companies from all industries. Therefore, it would also be exaggerated but correct to say that a product that doesn't have a social media presence isn't present in the lives of the users, either.

Social media marketing also plays an essential role in the success of purely physical retailers. Most customers research online before they even visit a store, which means that social media has an important influence on the purchase decision. There are two important strategies for achieving the right presence on social networks. The first one consists of actively presenting yourself as a brand. The second one involves customers of the brand sharing photos and selfies from the store.

Many small businesses have difficulty finding time to market themselves online. Therefore, it is even more important to consciously decide which social media platforms to invest time and money in. This is the only way the companies can really reach their own target customers.

Although Google My Business (GMB) is not a classic social media network, it is probably the most important platform for the self-portrayal of a business. Those interested can easily find information on your business in search queries, on maps, and on Google. You can upload images of your stores without a problem that show the shops at their best. This is free of charge and easy to manage.

© The Author(s) 2020
M. Spanke, *Retail Isn't Dead*, https://doi.org/10.1007/978-3-030-36650-6_9

Facebook is mainly an all-encompassing social media platform and certainly a good starting point for any business, regardless of the industry. It offers the physical retail market a lot of advertising opportunities. You can share photos, videos, and important company updates and encourage your customers to leave reviews on your site.

Instagram is an excellent option for products from the fashion, beauty, and food sectors that are visually appealing. It's primarily an app for sharing photos and is very popular with millennials in particular. It offers many opportunities to increase your brand recognition.

Twitter is a platform used by both business-to-consumer (B2C) and business-to-business (B2B) companies. It is suitable for news, trends, and customer concerns. Customers like to use Twitter when they have problems with a product or service by tweeting directly at the company. This can be a problem but also an opportunity, as everyone is able to see when companies react quickly and resolve the issue in real time.

Pinterest is like a pinboard full of ideas. If images and products are visually appealing, people often want to share them on their own digital pinboards. This medium is particularly suitable in the fashion, beauty, and living sectors. However, maintaining the account is a bit more complex.

Once you have decided which social platforms are the right ones for your business, then it is important to maintain them. It is recommended even for smaller businesses to nominate someone who will be responsible for this task. You can post products or campaign themes several times a day to networks like Instagram and Pinterest, as they are very visually oriented. Facebook and Twitter are good for new products, special offers, events, and targeted advertisements, among other things.

And now to the second strategy. Get your store "Social Media Ready." A basic prerequisite for your presence on social channels is an aesthetic store design that beckons customers to take photos and publish them. Create a selfie moment where every visitor feels the need to be photographed with the motif, without having to point it out to the customers. This focus point should be easily accessible so that selfies can be taken from many angles without a problem. Include brand hashtags in your displays and in the signage so that the images on the platforms can actually be associated with your store.

Lighting should not be too strong or too weak. If smartphone cameras require a flash, then the lighting is probably insufficient. Rule of thumb: Lighter photos get more likes than darker photos. Therefore, give your customers what they want, and you will get what you want.

Call to Action

- Consider which social media platforms are the best for you to reach your target group, and direct your energy and budget in a targeted manner. Be realistic and don't tackle all platforms at once.
- Nominate an employee on your team who will be responsible for social media.
- It is better to create one breathtaking selfie moment at the store than a lot of small selfie moments.
- Incorporate social media in the in-store advertising.

LINE FRIENDS: Selfie with a Plush Giant

LINE FRIENDS is a global character brand that originally started from BROWN & FRIENDS, created for use as stickers for LINE, the mobile messenger app that has over 164 million active users worldwide. They are used in various products, animations, games, cafes, hotels, and theme parks. There have been over 160 pop-ups and stores in 14 markets in cities such as New York, Los Angeles, London, Tokyo, Seoul and Shanghai. With its characters, LINE FRIENDS has showcased more than 6500 types of merchandise under wide categories such as toys, stationery, clothing, accessories, kids apparel, travel, interior and many more. The stores are 500 to 14,000 square feet in size and LINE FRIENDS mainly targets female consumers.

Image 9.1   LINE FRIENDS. (Source: LINE FRIENDS)

Stores and pop-ups from LINE FRIENDS are at locations with a very high tourist and customer frequency, which is ideal not only for selling merchandise articles at the stores. These locations are particularly suitable for strengthening brand development, brand experience, and brand awareness all around the cute characters.

There are countless selfie moments in the entire store. Right in the entrance area of each branch is a huge brown plush figure that is about ten feet tall. Each day of the week, customers line up to take a selfie with the character undisturbed. There are human-size characters all around the store, and the entire sales floor is laid out for photo opportunities. Often, the hashtags are mentioned at the same time. Signs saying, "Photos OK!" eliminate any doubt: Here, customers can and should take photos.

In addition to these selfie moments, there is naturally also a merchandise range that covers a large product line with articles from the popular LINE FRIENDS characters. The stores also sometimes offer exclusive products that are only available at physical retail stores and not part of the online assortment.

The calculation of LINE FRIENDS couldn't work out any better: Absolutely all customers stop at the stores to capture their moment with their smartphones. This shows how you can use social media for your brand through well-planned selfie moments.

Victoria's Secret: Happy Brand Ambassadors

Victoria's Secret is an American retail company for women's lingerie, women's fashion, and beauty products. The company was founded in San Francisco, California in 1977 and now belongs to L Brands Inc. The headquarters are in Columbus, Ohio. Victoria's Secret is one of the leading lingerie retailers in the United States. The company has more than 1100 stores worldwide.

When launching its fragrance range "Tease," Victoria's Secret set new standards in omnichannel marketing. Customers were asked via Instagram to visit a store and take a selfie while posing with their friends and a bottle of the fragrance. Whoever showed a store employee the posted photo on her smartphone with the hashtags #VSTease and #VSGift received a surprise gift.

As a result of this, Victoria's Secret not only increased its social media presence and attracted enthusiasm on Instagram but also increased customer frequency at the stores. At the same time, it was a good opportunity for the employees to connect with their customers in an entertaining way. In addition to the communication through Instagram, stickers were attached to the mirrors in order to draw attention to the selfie campaign.

So what is Victoria's secret? The answer is quite simple. A gift is sufficient for customers to take a quick photo of themselves and thus become brand ambassadors. Customers who see that kind of photo of their friends may feel inspired to visit the store themselves to do the same. This is how the marketing effect starts to multiply. Social media can be that easy to use.

H&M: Customers as Cover Models

Hennes & Mauritz AB is a Swedish chain store that offers fast-fashion apparel for women, men, young people, and children. The retailer was founded in Stockholm in 1947, where the headquarters are still located today. With over 170,000 employees and almost 4500 branches in more than 60 countries, H&M is the second largest clothing retailer in the world. The company's core target group involves fashionable and trendy consumers.

H&M focuses on innovations in customer retention in brick-and-mortar retail. The goal is to get customers excited about fashion, offer them fun, and create links between the offline and online experiences that are even stronger. A big step in this direction are the digital voice-controlled mirrors. They were introduced and installed for a limited period of time at one of the most famous and popular places in the world—on New York Times Square at the H&M flagship store.

The mirrors are distributed throughout the store and have a special type of facial recognition that is activated as soon as someone looks in the direction of a mirror for a sufficient period of time. A female voice is then heard that guides you through a menu. There are no touchscreens, buttons, or typing. This was done deliberately so that people using the new technology would not have any inhibitions or fears about making mistakes. There should be no uncertainty as to what the user has to do next.

The mirrors provide individualized styling recommendations, a direct link to e-commerce, and discounts via QR codes, and they invite customers to take selfies. The voice does a countdown so you can take a moment to prepare for the snapshot. But the technology of the "talking mirror" is not the only innovative and fascinating thing. The photos offer an experience as well that few customers would have had before. Whoever looks in the mirror and is photographed finds him or herself on the screen as the model of a magazine cover page. "Great cover" the mirror says enthusiastically, following which the selfie can be transferred directly to your own smartphone. The most important step then for H&M is for the photo to be shared on social media.

By implementing the mirrors, the company achieved its goal: Offline is linked to online in an uncomplicated and entertaining way. In doing so, H&M cleverly advertises on the social media of its customers.

Bibliography

Baron, Katie. 2018. Ambient Tech That Actually Works: H&M Launches A Voice Activated Mirror. *Forbes.* https://www.forbes.com/sites/katiebaron/2018/06/07/ambient-tech-that-actually-works-hm-launches-a-voice-activated-mirror/#6233e5bd4463.

Hendriksz, Vivian. 2015. Victoria's Secret Puts Selfies in the Spotlight with New Campaign. *FashionUnited.* https://fashionunited.uk/news/fashion/victoria-s-secret-puts-selfies-in-the-spotlight-with-new-campaign/2015081817385.

Samuely, Alex. Victoria's Secret Unclasps Selfies In-store Potential. https://www.retaildive.com/ex/mobilecommercedaily/victorias-secret-unclasps-new-marketing-method-with-in-store-selfie-activations.

10

In-Store Apps

Retailers deal with their apps in very different ways. Some just try to replicate their online store, while others use the apps primarily for advertising purposes or don't even have an app. In brick-and-mortar retail, digital applications have limited use. However, there are countless possibilities and opportunities for everything these individually programmed software applications on your customers' smartphones can offer—you and especially your consumers.

Over half the people who use a retail app use it when shopping at a physical store. This is your chance to improve the shopping experience, establish customer retention, and increase store sales. After all, there is no better time to be connected with the customers than when they are already at the store. The good thing about this is that only software has to be provided, no hardware, as every customer already has that in the pants pocket, namely, a smartphone.

Apps can be used to provide product-related information. This ranges from price comparisons and detailed product descriptions to product reviews. At the same time, an app also presents the opportunity to make in-store offers to customers or to provide exclusive promotions for the store visit. This is particularly interesting if the app uses the cell phone's location technology. Individual products can be offered based on location. If a fashion store customer happens to be standing in front of the jeans section, for example, he or she is recommended the latest jeans fit or wash look right away. And if he or she immediately accepts the recommendation, there may be a discount as well.

The app can use the location technology to turn into something like an in-store navigation device. It guides the customer directly to the right row of shelves to the desired product—quickly, conveniently, and without any detours. Especially in larger stores, this navigation is of enormous benefit to customers.

© The Author(s) 2020
M. Spanke, *Retail Isn't Dead*, https://doi.org/10.1007/978-3-030-36650-6_10

The mobile checkout process is also an important aspect of an app to improve the in-store experience, allowing customers to just pay via the app. But customers aren't the only ones who have a cell phone here. Especially during rush hour, it makes sense for sales employees to be equipped with smartphones and for software to turn the devices into mobile checkouts. This allows customers to pay directly through the employee on the sales floor, without having to line up at the checkout.

With apps, you can collect a vast amount of customer information just like it's done with online shopping. This includes navigation via the app, products selected, purchases made, and the buying behavior at the store. Companies can utilize all this information to optimize the shopping experience and to personalize offers for customers. After all, those who understand their customers have the big advantage of being able to offer them products in a targeted manner that as a result of this knowledge will probably arouse their interest.

These are just a few examples of the many possibilities that in-store apps offer. With their help, you can connect with customers before, during, and after the store visit. You can make their shopping experience more efficient and exciting. It is always important that they are offered added value. With many apps, the potentials were often not even partially exhausted.

Call to Action

- An app can have two main goals: to increase customer frequency or to improve the in-store experience. Consider if you want to pursue one goal, the other, or both.
- Define what about the shopping experience bothers your customers and how an app can solve this problem.
- Don't just try to offer a lot of features but concentrate on what really offers the customer added value.

The Home Depot: My Personal Assistant

The Home Depot Inc. is the largest DIY chain worldwide and employs almost 400,000 workers. The company was founded in 1978 and has its headquarters in Atlanta in the US state of Georgia. It has more than 2200 stores in the United States, Canada, and Mexico. The average sales area of these stores is almost 105,000 square feet, where products for do-it-yourselfers and professional building contractors are offered.

We all know the greatest pain points in shopping at a hardware store: The desired articles either can't be found or are not available. If you look for an employee, then you often don't find one or this person is responsible for another department. That means: Tough luck, keep looking! Home Depot has taken care of these pain points in the customer experience and developed an award-winning app. The goal was to offer customers useful tools on their smartphones and to create an interlinked online-offline experience.

The app can be used at home already to search for desired items using the integrated voice control. It is also possible to check which of the nearest stores have these articles available. If something isn't working at home and needs to be replaced, just take a photo of it. Through the integrated image search, a list of similar articles is instantly displayed. Now you can take the digital shopping list with you to the nearest store where the merchandise is available. Alternatively, the "Buy Online, Pickup in Store" service can be used right away, which has the merchandise available within two hours. All this is possible through the app.

But there is more. When you arrive at the store with your digital shopping list, the app shows you exactly the aisle and shelving unit where the desired articles are presented. With the app's barcode scanner, you get detailed information on the product or can read customer reviews. If you are still unsure, an online employee is available via the live chat to answer any questions.

The app is used to provide customers with instructions, advice on DIY projects, or tips on furnishing and decorating. Through an augmented reality feature, an article can be selected and optically integrated into the scanned image of a room. This allows you to see directly on the smartphone whether the objects optically suit the interior at home.

The app works as if you had your own personal DIY store employee at your side who can answer any question. There are all kinds of information via the app on all available articles—40,000 at the store, more than one million online. The application is easy to use, solves various customer problems, and saves time, money, and especially nerves.

Nike: The Perfect Flow

Nike Inc. is a multinational company with its head office in the greater Portland area of the US state of Oregon. Founded in 1964, the sports brand has almost 1200 stores worldwide and is sold by retail partners in more than 30,000 locations. Nike employs more than 70,000 workers worldwide to design, develop, manufacture, and sell shoes, apparel, equipment, and accessories. The core target group involves consumers between the ages of 15 and 40.

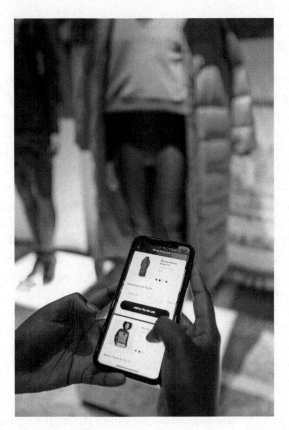

Image 10.1   Nike. (Source: Nike)

The Nike app was developed based on customer surveys. Nike wanted to know what consumers like and dislike about store visits. The result was that customers want to be able to know in advance whether or not the sneakers they want are available at the nearest store. The same applies to the store: Customers want to find the products themselves and help themselves, without having to speak to a store employee if they don't feel like it. These and many other options were integrated into the Nike app to provide a smooth and positive in-store experience.

The shopping experience starts at home already, when you can use the app to search for a certain article and check if it is available at the store in the right size. If so, it can simply be reserved, and in less than two hours, it is ready for pickup. As soon as the merchandise can be received, you are informed of this via a push notification. A password is sent to your smartphone, with which you can open a locker at the store containing the desired articles. Nike makes it that easy.

In order to be able to use these and other services, you have to be a Nike member. Membership is free of charge and offers a lot of benefits. The geolocation tagging feature allows the app to recognize when the customer enters the store. Following this, the app sends the consumer push messages about exclusive discounts or bonus programs.

At the store, the customer decides if he or she wants self-service or an advisory service. At select Nike stores, there is also a chat feature with the option of "messaging" shop employees on site instead of speaking to someone personally. Young customers in particular make use of this option, as they often prefer not to interact with sales staff.

The app's barcode scan feature can be used to retrieve further product information and available sizes and colors in real time. Through the online connection to sales staff, the desired article is simply requested and brought to any location at the store. At a New York branch, customers can even scan a complete mannequin and have the entire outfit brought to a fitting room in the requested size.

Once an article has been chosen, regardless of whether it was provided in a locker for pickup or found at the store just now, it can be paid for directly with the app's instant checkout feature, without the lines at the checkout. There could hardly be any more flow.

The data and information collected through the app with regard to customers' purchasing behavior in the region are analyzed and provided to the store teams. This allows predictions to be made on what is likely to sell well.

With this app, Nike has managed to perfectly link the digital shopping experience with the physical one. What is its secret to success? The company listened closely to its customers and eliminated the disruptive factors in the shopping experience.

7FRESH: The App Does It All

The Chinese fresh food supermarket concept 7FRESH has been around since 2018. The supermarkets, which have an average size of around 3000 to 4000 square feet, offer an omnichannel gourmet fresh food experience combining "supermarket + dining + lifestyle", providing consumers not only fresh, safe and reliable products, but also the opportunity to dine in store. More than 70 percent items in 7FRESH are fresh products. The chain store belongs to JD.com, which was founded in 1998 and is a Chinese e-commerce company with its headquarters in Beijing. JD is the largest retailer in China, online or offline.

Image 10.2   7FRESH. (Source: 7FRESH)

7FRESH positions itself as a lifestyle brand, focusing on product transparency and customer service through the support of technology. Due to the food scandals of recent years, people in China have largely lost their trust in food suppliers. In order to regain this trust while providing education to customers about healthy choices, 7FRESH makes a point of disclosing all product information down to the smallest detail at its stores with the help of its own app.

Those wanting to shop at 7FRESH must first download the app. It is used to scan all items, activate the informative displays, and to also pay for all the purchases. At the same time, non-sensitive customer data related to purchasing behavior that are collected this way are used to provide personalized product recommendations through the app.

Since customers here are so sensitive when it comes to handling food, even fresh products on the markets like fruit and vegetables are packaged. This is another point that sets 7FRESH apart from other businesses. Here, technology comes into play again. If, for example, a customer grabs an apple that has been sealed in foil and scans the bar code on the shelf, all information on this product appears on a digital display. This ranges from the ingredients to the business of origin and sugar content to customer reviews.

Pricing is displayed on electronic price tags, which are synchronized with the online prices and can easily be adjusted with one click. After all, the omnichannel concept stipulates that customers can select products from the comfort of their homes, and have them delivered in one click in as fast as

30 minutes, or make purchases directly from the store. The reason: It is proven that customers who purchase both online and offline spend more money. That's why multichannel customers are so popular with companies. Payment happens almost exclusively over cell phones. Cash and credit card payments are accepted, giving visitors from out of town who might not have access to mobile payment methods a chance to enjoy products from the store.

Through the app, 7FRESH provides its customers with all information on its products, without flooding the entire store with signs and information.

Bibliography

Conaway, Cameron. 2018. Could JD.com's 7FRESH Set New Benchmarks for Supermarkets in Asia?. https://www.huffpost.com/entry/could-jdcoms-7fresh-set-new-benchmarks-for-supermarkets_b_5a53dc9de4b0f9b24bf319d4?guccounter=1&guce_referrer=aHR0cHM6Ly93d3cuZ29vZ2xlLmNvbS8&guce_referrer_sig=AQAAANjuDCBDzTNHVZ4_oTcO1NNE7Ls1AOYmwVqxUYJ5t8mgVy-fxiRXVJc7D7WVlNdgIlZRrHMTmPQLWAX6RIEhltRsOItYGjvaR3ym5soFL_qotMIsQjru1rAkq5eBDxSe3MfNGth5Jx-2WMj4CD6LMmlbHKsT6yhiGC-C3jDKXsTQgp.

Nike. 2018. Breaking Down the Nike App at Retail. https://news.nike.com/news/nike-app-at-retail-shopping-experience.

The Home Depot. 2018. 5 Technologies Changing How We Shop. https://corporate.homedepot.com/newsroom/forrester-rates-home-depots-mobile-app-1-retail.

———. 2019. Forrester Rates the Home Depot's Mobile App #1 in Retail. https://corporate.homedepot.com/newsroom/forrester-rates-home-depots-mobile-app-1-retail.

11

Easy Checkout

E-commerce means that articles can be searched for and found with great ease and speed. The payment process is just as easy and quick. Online purchases are confirmed and paid for in seconds with a click, fingerprint, or by facial recognition. This increases customers' expectations of a quick and smooth shopping experience. After all, in an era where any consumer can get everything at once, customers have less and less patience for lengthy payment processes. This has consequences for brick-and-mortar retailers: You have to adapt and make the payment process more convenient, smoother, and, above all, faster for customers.

The greatest potential for saving time, however, is not the payment process at the checkout but the navigation at the store. Realistically speaking, customers primarily look for products they need at the moment; most of the products from the overall range are of no interest to them at this point. This means that locating the desired products quickly should come before the easy payment. If a customer knows exactly which article he or she wants, then it should be possible for him or her to combine shopping and payment into one quick experience. An example of this involves having a separate area at a store where the most commonly purchased everyday articles are made available to customers with little time, preferably combined with self-checkout kiosks.

Today, most customers pay by credit card or with the pay function of their smartphones. Therefore, it makes sense to equip employees with portable cash register systems. This allows a sales employee to accompany customers throughout the entire process of greeting and advising them to the final payment. This is already the case at many Nike and Apple stores.

© The Author(s) 2020
M. Spanke, *Retail Isn't Dead*, https://doi.org/10.1007/978-3-030-36650-6_11

Self-checkout systems are becoming more and more popular. Simply scan, purchase, pack, and leave. They are available now at retailers of all industries and price segments. Thus, a self-checkout system was also implemented at the New York store of the luxury brand Rebecca Minkoff. Since that might not appeal to everyone, a combination of two alternatives may be the best solution: regular checkouts for customers who prefer personal contact and self-checkout systems for customers in a hurry.

In addition, there are various Scan & Go systems that work by means of an app of the respective company. This turns the smartphone into a scanner with which all products are scanned and paid for directly by the customer. In addition, there are several other concepts like Checkout Free, where you simply help yourself to the products and are billed automatically through the customer account with the company.

All these solutions are only about one thing: saving customers time and making things as convenient as possible for them.

Call to Action

- Concentrate on what will help customers the most during the checkout process.
- Consider exactly which checkout solutions are most suitable for and most likely to be accepted by your customers. After all, not all technology solutions are suitable for every customer.
- Ask yourself if fast checkout processes really add value for your customers or whether the lack of interaction with people leads to an inferior shopping experience.

Target: Dual Speed—Quick or Inspiring?

Target Corporation was founded in 1962 in Minneapolis, where the headquarters are still located today. With over 350,000 employees and more than 1850 stores, Target is the eighth largest retailer in the USA. The discount store with an average of 130,000 square feet offers food, cosmetics, clothing, and household and electrical appliances. The average age of its customers is 40, and their annual household income is between 60,000 and 70,000 US dollars.

The big-box retailer Target has surveyed its customers to identify their individual needs at various locations. What do the respective neighborhoods need the most? The customer is the focus of this survey and the concepts resulting from it. One of the individual concepts that emerged from this is the dual design principles to make stores both easy and inspiring to shop. Stores across the country have elements for both who are in a hurry and customers who want to leisurely stroll through the aisles and browse. And in some stores with two entrances, the store is designed to offer one side of shopping for quick convenience, and the other side for inspiration and discovery.

If customers use the "Inspiration" entrance, they are guided through the entire store, and as previously mentioned, we are talking about an average of 130,000 square feet. Conversely, if customers choose the "Ease" entrance, they encounter grab-and-go groceries, wine, beer, and a selection of everyday items like at convenience stores. The point here is to offer the customers the essentials so that they can quickly and easily remove shopping from their to-do list. Self-checkout stations are available for fast payment.

Online orders are paid for directly through the website or smartphone and made available for pickup within an hour. These can then be received at the pickup counter in the "Ease" area. Those in a real hurry use the "Drive Up" service. For this, too, you order your merchandise online. Once it is available to be picked up, the customers give notification when they are leaving for the pickup and then again when they have arrived in the designated parking area. Target employees then come out, load the cars, and the customers are already on their way again. It really doesn't get any faster than that.

The "Ease" concept solves the problem many customers have: lack of time. The solution is applied at all levels of the shopping process.

Zara: Try on, Pack, and Leave

Zara SA is a Spanish fast-fashion retailer that belongs to one of the world's largest clothing retailer, the Inditex Group. The company, which was founded in 1975, has 2250 stores in almost 100 markets. It is known for its highly responsive supply chain. Once the products have been designed, they only need ten to fifteen days to get to the stores. With its selection of women's, men's, and children's clothing, the company is aimed at women and men who are very interested in the latest fashion trends.

Self-checkout stations are already widespread at supermarkets, but they are still rarely seen in fashion retail. This is surprising, as customers here would also like a quick and convenient shopping experience.

At Zara in London, this is already a possibility. Here, the convenience of online shopping in terms of payment is transferred to the in-store experience. It is just as easy to shop at this store as it is to shop online, with the advantage that you can try on merchandise and take it with you right away. A touchscreen surface guides you through the fast payment process. The clothing item isn't scanned; rather, it is simply held close to the checkout station, and the product and price immediately appear on the display. Then you can pay, and the security tag can be removed. Thus, the entire process is unusually fast and smooth.

We often take all the time in the world to try things on, but paying can't be fast enough. Thus, this form of service is perfect for customers, as the wait times at the cash registers are eliminated.

Marks & Spencer: High Speed Shopping During the Break

Marks & Spencer Group plc, also known as M&S, is a British retailer with its headquarters in London. The company, which was founded in 1884, employs more than 80,000 workers and has more than 1400 stores worldwide, over 1000 of which are in Great Britain. The product range includes apparel, cosmetics, household goods, and food.

Image 11.1   Marks & Spencer. (Source: Marks & Spencer)

During lunchtime, the lines at the many Marks & Spencer's grocery stores are the longest. In order to eliminate this flaw in the customer experience, M&S has launched "Mobile, Pay, Go." How does the app work, and how does it solve the problem?

In order to use this service, you download the M&S mobile app first and activate the M&S loyalty program. During registration, the payment options are selected. The system accepts debit or credit cards as well as Apple Pay or Google Pay.

The app recognizes when a customer enters a store and automatically activates the "Mobile, Pay, Go" function. The smartphone's camera then turns into a mobile scanner with which you can directly scan the barcodes from the goods or shelves. Scanned products are immediately added to the app's shopping cart. Payment can be made from anywhere in the store, and the app uses your fingerprint or facial recognition for identification. The receipt is sent to the smartphone as a QR code. So easy, so convenient.

This service allows customers to scan and pay for articles in less than 40 seconds. The app is particularly useful at stores where a high percentage of shopping is done during lunchtime. Customers come during their usually short break, which is at a time when the store is busiest. "Mobile, Pay, Go" is thus perfect for customers with narrow timing.

Albert Heijn: Tap to Go

Albert Heijn BV is the largest Dutch supermarket chain and was founded in 1887. The company employs over 100,000 workers and operates more than 950 stores across the Netherlands and Belgium. Albert Heijn's parent company is Ahold Delhaize, the owner of U.S. supermarket chains like Stop & Shop, Food Lion and Giant Food Stores. *The size of Albert Heijn stores varies by format. Albert Heijn's mission is to be the supermarket for everybody.*

Image 11.2   Albert Heijn. (Source: Albert Heijn)

Wouldn't it be fantastic to go to a supermarket, bag whatever you like, and leave the store without paying at the checkout, and legally? This is possible at Albert Heijn in Zaadem. The store doesn't have a single checkout, and customers don't even have to take their smartphone out of their pocket in order to pay.

Customers register for the program "Tap to Go" and receive a card with a payment function that is directly connected to the customer's bank account. You don't check in when entering a store, so that you can start shopping right away. When selecting an item, you simply tap the electronic shelf label underneath with the personal card, and the label lights up green at the edges. You take the merchandise and continue shopping. Each tag or shelf label shows the price and barcode of the respective article. Customers now have ten minutes to reverse their decision and return the article. In this case, you tap the shelf label again, which then lights up red at the edges. If that isn't done, the purchase is finalized after ten minutes.

This concept is ideal at convenience stores, where time is of the essence. At train stations, for example, this technology is perfect for customers, as there are no wait times in spite of high customer frequency. Even people who are in a hurry can shop for the upcoming train ride in a matter of seconds.

In terms of turnover, "Tap to Go" has great potential for customers with impulsive buying behavior. Without cash registers, customers are less capable of resisting the temptations at the store. In addition, you only have limited time to change your mind. The electronic shelf tags are connected to the software system and thus present the possibility of dynamic prices. Just like hotel prices, they can be adjusted according to supply and demand.

The lack of checkouts, however, also means that this space can be used for further products and staff costs can be reduced.

Incidentally, this system also gives Albert Heijn access to detailed data on the buying behavior of its customers: what paths they take when moving around, which items they select in which order, which products are their individual favorite ones, and much more. This information can be used to optimize product placement in the entire store and to offer the respective card holder individually tailored product suggestions.

The "Tap to Go" system is very convenient for customers, saves time, and also has a lot of advantages for the company to keep a few steps ahead of competitors both online and offline.

Amazon Go: Shopping with an AI Camera

Amazon is the world's largest e-commerce business and has its headquarters in the US state of Washington. It was founded in 1994 and currently employs around 650,000 workers. The first Amazon Go store was opened to the public in Seattle in 2018. As of October 2019, there are around 16 of these stores now open in the USA. The 1800-square-foot store offers all kinds of items—from pre-made sandwiches, salads, snacks, and drinks to essential groceries and traditional ready-made meals. With this concept, Amazon Go is a convenient way for customers to grab great food fast.

Image 11.3 Amazon Go. (Source: BIG IDEAS Visual Merchandising Inc)

The Amazon Go shop itself is like a normal convenience store, but the technology is unique. Here, articles aren't scanned, and there are no checkouts. You come, take the merchandise, and leave again. It's that simple, which is why Amazon calls it "Just Walk Out Technology."

Customers download the Amazon Go app and link it to their Amazon account. When entering the store, the smartphone is held up against a scanner in the entrance area with the app open. Then the cell phone is placed back in the pocket, and you can start shopping.

Everything you want to buy is then placed into bags that you have either brought or are provided at the store. The "Just Walk Out Technology" detects exactly what the customers are taking from the shelves and keeps track of them in a virtual shopping cart, just like on the Amazon website. If a customer returns an item back to the shelves, it is removed from the virtual shopping cart. Upon leaving the store, the system charges your Amazon account and generates a receipt that can be retrieved though the app.

What is behind this? The technology that enables this checkout-free shopping experience is a combination of computer vision, sensor fusion, and deep learning. This type of technology is also used in driverless cars. Incredibly precise technology is required to implement the Amazon Go concept. After all, steps are taken as a matter of course to make sure that customers only pay for what they actually take with them.

It doesn't matter how much of a hurry the customer is in, shopping here is always possible. Customers can enter the store, fill their bags, and leave the store again in a short time. There are never any wait times for the customer during this shopping experience. This system also offers the highest degree of convenience at this time.

The retail experience is being redefined for Amazon Go customers. For Amazon, this is another test area to learn even more about customer behavior in brick-and-mortar retail. In addition to the standard information on the customers themselves, all kinds of data are available for each product offered. How often is a product touched, and how often is it put back? How long does it take the customer to put it back? Which product does the customer choose as an alternative? The list of questions and answers could be continued indefinitely. This knowledge can give Amazon a big advantage in offline trading as well.

Bibliography

Amazon. Amazon Go. https://www.amazon.com/b?ie=UTF8&node=16008589011.
Badoim, Lana. 2018. Cashierless Shopping with 'Tap To Go' Technology Is Coming to More Grocery Stores. *Forbes.* https://www.forbes.com/sites/lanabandoim/2018/09/26/cashierless-shopping-with-tap-to-go-technology-is-coming-to-more-grocery-stores/#7220d54b5f05.
Cheng, Andria. 2019. Why Amazon Go May Soon Change the Way We Shop. *Forbes.* https://www.forbes.com/sites/andriacheng/2019/01/13/why-amazon-go-may-soon-change-the-way-we-want-to-shop/#238ad7670977.
Diner, Jessica. 2017. Help Yourself: How Zara Is Elevating the Self-Service Experience. *Vogue.*https://www.vogue.co.uk/article/zara-self-service-checkout-shopping-review-fast-fashion.
Howell, David. 2018. Mobile, Pay, Go: We're Enabling More Customers to Experience the Checkout Free Checkout. Marks & Spencer. https://corporate.marksandspencer.com/stories/blog/mobile-pay-go-we-re-enabling-more-customers-to-experience-the-checkout-free-checkout.

Inditex. 2018. Zara Stratford Flagship Store Pioneers New Approach to Integrating Stores and Online. https://www.inditex.com/article?articleId=569282&title=Zara+Stratford+flagship+store+pioneers+new+approach++to+integrating+stores+and+online.

Marks & Spencer. 2018. M&S Rolls Out Checkout Free Checkout as Part of Digital First Strategy. https://corporate.marksandspencer.com/media/press-releases/2018/m-and-s-rolls-out-checkout-free-checkout-as-part-of-digital-first-strategy.

Sharma, Amit. 2019. How Target Got Its 'Tar-jay' Back by Thinking Beyond Channels. *Retail Dive*. https://www.retaildive.com/news/how-target-got-its-tar-jay-back-by-thinking-beyond-channels/547963/.

Stratton, Lauren. 2018. My Role in the Digital Transformation: Mobile, Pay, Go. Marks & Spencer. https://corporate.marksandspencer.com/stories/blog/my-role-in-the-digital-transformation-mobile-pay-go.

Target. 2017. Target Reveals Design Elements of Next Generation of Stores. https://corporate.target.com/press/releases/2017/03/target-reveals-design-elements-of-next-generation.

12

Pickup and Returns

High shipping costs for online orders are a problem for companies. Today, customers just expect merchandise to be delivered and returned free of charge. To remain competitive, companies inevitably have to agree to this. However, if a company has a lot of physical retail locations, this can be an advantage. After all, the dispatch and return of online orders on site is an excellent way to cut shipping costs.

An added bonus for customers is that the merchandise is often available for pickup within an hour and they don't have to wait for it to be delivered home. If it suddenly occurs to us on December 23rd that Christmas is almost here, then it's high time for last-minute Christmas shopping. For most online services, it's already too late then for a prompt delivery. However, ordering merchandise online and picking it up at the store still allows enough time even to calmly wrap the gifts.

A further advantage in these situations that shouldn't be underestimated in brick-and-mortar retail is that if a customer has already been to the store to pick up or return merchandise, he or she will possibly do more shopping. This in any case increases customer frequency, which means a greater chance of generating further sales.

Another strategy is "Buy Online Send to Store," which basically works just the same, except that the merchandise isn't taken from the branch's inventory but is sent to the shop.

Some companies have a separate counter where the ordered items can be picked up. However, there is an element of risk here for a positive customer experience: Sometimes, there are several customers wanting to pick up their merchandise at the same time, which incurs wait times. This is an important

© The Author(s) 2020
M. Spanke, *Retail Isn't Dead*, https://doi.org/10.1007/978-3-030-36650-6_12

factor that online customers want to avoid. That is why a lot of stores have implemented pickup lockers or automated pickup systems. As soon as customers enter the store, they simply scan their order codes at a machine, and a locker opens, allowing them to take the merchandise.

Many companies are even going one step further by offering their customers "Curbside Pickup." The merchandise is delivered directly to the parked car in front of the store. This works the same way as "Buy Online, Pickup in Store"— with a difference: By clicking on your smartphone, you indicate that you are leaving for the pickup at that time. With an additional click, you indicate that you have arrived in front of the store. Sales employees then hurry to the curbside pickup parking space and load the car with the articles purchased.

Many online buyers place orders with the intention of returning at least part of the order. If stores try to manage online returns in addition to those of the shops using the same processes, it generally won't work. The result is that customer wait times will increase and definitely won't lead to a positive experience. But if articles can be returned in a quick and simple manner, retailers can gain loyal customers. In this case, just as with the pickup service, there are automated return stations as well. These work in a similar way and offer the convenience and speed that not only online customers want.

One might think that it would be a clever idea to move the pickup and returns counters to the back of the store. That way, customers would have to pass a lot of merchandise on their way there, which would increase sales opportunities. This is definitely the wrong strategy, however. Most online customers choose the digital version of shopping in order to save time. If customers have to walk a long way to exchange or return purchases, retailers will be at a disadvantage compared with online trading. Another argument against this strategy: Who says that having pickup and return counters directly at the entrance reduces the chance of additional sales?

If companies offer a pickup and return service, customers and the businesses will benefit from it in many ways, but under one condition: It has to be done right.

Call to Action

- Clarify how you can offer a fast and simple pickup and return service.
- Adapt your processes so that the ordered merchandise is sent from the warehouse to the pickup station and from there to the customer in a short time.
- Provide a specific pickup and return area at an easily accessible and recognizable point near the entrance.

Nordstrom: Pickup in the District

Nordstrom Inc. is an American luxury department store chain with its headquarters in Seattle in the US State of Washington. Founded in 1901, the company employs over 70,000 workers and has nearly 400 stores in the USA and Canada. Nordstrom carries apparel, accessories, shoes, cosmetics, and fragrances. At select stores, there are also departments for wedding attire and furnishings.

Imagine that your favorite fashion store has no stock but nonetheless has more to offer than any other shop. This most likely will be Nordstrom Local, a so-called service hub in the neighborhood. Here, online orders can be picked up or returned. There is a personal styling service, a tailor's shop, a cleaning service, nail care, and much more. The goal is to become part of the local community. A place where customers drop in briefly on their way home from work, maybe to pick up their online order or even to try on the merchandise right away.

In order to tailor the services precisely to the specific needs of each neighborhood, Nordstrom needs to know its customers well in the individual districts. The point is to understand what they want and which services may not be available yet in their community. In any case, there is one thing that all Nordstrom Local stores have in common: There is either no inventory at all or few curated products; and there are various pickup and return services at all the locations.

"Buy Online, Pickup in Store" is an integral part of Nordstrom Local. It's quite simple: Select an article online, click on "Shop Your Store," and choose a Nordstrom Local. The order is ready for pickup the same day and the customer will be notified by email.

If you don't have time for all this, you use "Curbside Pickup," i.e., delivery right to your own car. When you leave for the pickup, just click on "On My Way." Upon arriving at the curbside pickup area in front of the store, stop and click on "I'm Here," and your order is delivered to your car.

Returns are just as fast and simple. Each store employee can accept these without a problem. Even returns for other retailers are accepted here, regardless of where or with whom the order was placed online. If the vendor does not offer a free return service, Nordstrom Local also pays the shipping costs for a lump sum of five dollars. As soon as the merchandise to be returned is on its way, the customer receives an email with the shipping number.

With Nordstrom Local, the best of online and offline shopping is united. The convenience and speed are associated with the shopping experience and personal contact. Thus, customers no longer see Nordstrom as a website or local store but as a combination of the two.

Walmart: "Pickup Tower" for XL Purchases

Walmart Inc. is a US retail group operating a chain of consumer markets, discounters, and grocery stores. Founded in 1962, the company is the largest grocer in the USA and at the same time the company with the highest revenue in the world. Walmart operates 11,000 stores in 27 countries under 55 different names. With 2.2 million employees, it is the largest private employer in the world. The average store size is around 175,000 square feet.

Image 12.1   Walmart. (Source: Walmart)

At Walmart, customers receive a discount when they pick up their online orders at the nearest store instead of having them delivered home. Sending merchandise to its own stores is much cheaper for Walmart than sending it directly to customers. This is a smart move to gain an advantage over other online providers. The competitor Amazon offers its customer's pickup lockers, but they are restricted in size, whereas Walmart customers can even have a TV delivered to the "Pickup Tower."

Walmart currently has about 1700 of these "Pickup Towers" at its stores. They are always positioned in a central location at the entrance so that customers can pick up the merchandise quickly. With a height of around 16 feet and a width of approximately one and a five feet, the pickup stations are impossible to overlook. As soon as you have completed your online purchase and received the pickup code on your smartphone, you just hold the code against the tower's scanner at the store. Within ten to a maximum of 45 seconds, the tower's delivery drawer lights up and opens. The products that have been ordered and paid for can be removed.

Walmart also has almost 2500 pickup lockers for groceries. By the end of 2020, over 3000 locations are expected to have "Curbside Pickup." Here, the merchandise ordered online will be delivered directly to the Walmart parking lot and loaded into the car by employees.

Returns are another challenge. Whenever you want to exchange something, you stand in line with other customers waiting to do the same thing. Walmart has also developed a concept for this dilemma that offers its customers a simple and smooth return service. The so-called "Mobile Express Returns" are available at almost 5000 locations. All you have to do is open the Walmart app, select the purchased item, click on "Mobile Express Returns," and after a few more clicks, a confirmation code appears on your smartphone. With this, you head straight to the "Mobile Express Lane," a shopping lane dedicated to this service, scan the QR code, and hand the merchandise to the employee. The credit is issued the next day.

When it comes to pickup and returns, the Walmart concepts have definitely been developed from a customer's perspective. Simple, convenient, and quick, exactly what is expected today.

Kohl's: Growing with Amazon Returns

Kohl's Corporation is an omnichannel retailer that first opened in 1962. The headquarters are located in Menomonee Falls, Wisconsin today. The current chain consists of more than 1150 store locations in the USA and employs around 130,000 workers. The stores, which have an average size of 85,000 square feet, sell proprietary and national brand apparel, footwear, accessories, beauty and home products. The core target group involves women between the ages of 35 and 55 with a medium income who shop for the whole family.

When it comes to returns, Kohl's has come up with a clever idea, thinking outside the box. The department store chain has entered into a partnership with Amazon and offers the return of Amazon packages at all of its more than 1150 Kohl's locations. Here, articles are even accepted without a box or label. They are packaged for the customer at no extra cost and then returned to one of Amazon's return centers. Why? In order to direct additional customer traffic into its own stores. The return process is quite simple. The return of an article is entered on the Amazon account, and "Kohl's Dropoff" is selected as the return location. The customer is then recommended the nearest Kohl's branch where the merchandise can be dropped off. Those who want to can package the item and print out the label themselves.

Those who don't feel like doing this can still return the merchandise, as it will be accepted. There are Amazon return parking spaces directly in front of the drop-off door. At the store, the label is scanned for the customer, and the merchandise is accepted. In addition, each customer dropping off an Amazon package receives a discount voucher for 25 percent. Customer convenience is thus rewarded on top of everything else.

All these concepts help Amazon reduce the rising costs of returns, as today, customers just expect returns to be free of charge. For Kohl's, this cooperation means increased customer frequency, making this cooperation a win-win situation for both partners.

Bibliography

Kohl's. 2019. Service Offers a Free, Convenient Experience for Customers. https://corporate.kohls.com/news/archive-/2019/july/kohl-s-now-accepts-amazon-returns-at-all-stores-.

Maheshwari, Sapna. 2019. Kohl's Is Betting on Amazon Returns to Drive Sales. *The New York Times*. https://www.nytimes.com/2019/07/08/business/kohls-amazon-returns.html.

Nordstrom. 2018. Nordstrom Local. https://shop.nordstrom.com/c/nordstrom-local.

———. 2018. Nordstrom Local Expands in Los Angeles. https://press.nordstrom.com/news-releases/news-release-details/nordstrom-local-expands-los-angeles.

Walmart. 2018. Hundreds More High-Tech Pickup Towers Are Headed Your Way. https://corporate.walmart.com/newsroom/innovation/20180405/hundreds-more-high-tech-pickup-towers-are-headed-your-way.

13

Delivery

It doesn't matter whether it's food, groceries, books, TVs, or whatever—anything can be ordered at any time and delivered home. The percentage of retail turnover from online sales is constantly on the rise. Today, the boundary between digital and physical retail is becoming more blurred than ever before. As a result, customers also increasingly expect retailers to deliver anything at any time. The delivery service will continue to play an increasingly important role in the future. As a consequence, retailers have to develop new and fast delivery strategies that satisfy on-demand customers but are still affordable. This service not only serves to meet the wishes and convenience of customers but offers companies the opportunity to differentiate themselves from the competition through the service.

Retailers can use their numerous branches as warehouses for the delivery of online purchases. Since e-commerce companies usually ship their orders from large warehouses near important hubs that are not necessarily close to customers, the delivery can sometimes take a few days. This situation can lead to an advantage for brick-and-mortar retailers, specifically if thanks to the high area density of their stores, they can deliver the merchandise within a day or even within a few hours. Physical locations can thus utilize their inventory to serve digital customers, which not only shortens delivery times but also reduces delivery costs.

The more deliveries are made, the greater the environmental impact is, and customers are aware of this. Against the background of the public debate on environmental sustainability, the number of these customers has been growing particularly fast and strongly in recent years. Sustainable delivery options will, therefore, become a decisive factor for purchase decisions in the medium

© The Author(s) 2020
M. Spanke, *Retail Isn't Dead*, https://doi.org/10.1007/978-3-030-36650-6_13

term. With a view to this situation, online and offline retailers worldwide are testing various delivery strategies—from electric vehicles to bike couriers.

There are no longer any limits to the destination of deliveries, either. At airports like in Dubai or Amsterdam, there is already a delivery service that brings food orders directly to the gate. Amazon even offers the owners of General Motors vehicles in the USA delivery directly into a parked car. As soon as the delivery person arrives at the vehicle, he sends a request through his Amazon scanner for the car to be unlocked remotely. Amazon compares the given vehicle with the order, authorizes the delivery, and unlocks the car via GMC Connected Services. The package is deposited, the delivery person locks the car again, and the customer receives a delivery confirmation.

In China, a luxury retailer has merchandise delivered to its best customers only in beautifully packaged parcels by delivery drivers dressed completely in white, who drive up in a premium black vehicle. This is also an opportunity to distinguish yourself from competitors by a consistent brand experience.

There are many more options that are being tested in this context. From delivery with robots or drones to groceries being delivered directly into the fridge when no one is home. There are a lot of indications that the latest forms of delivery will not become commonplace in the near future. However, a look back shows how even innovations that take a lot of time to get used to can be taken for granted over time. In the '90s, despite all reservations, consumers had to get used to online credit card payments. Today, this version of processing a payment is taken for granted.

The delivery service can become a distinguishing feature between you and your competitors. Whether through speed, additional services during delivery, or through a consistently convenient shopping experience from the selection to the purchase to delivery to the customer's home.

Call to Action

- Ask yourself what added value your customers have through the delivery and whether there may be a special service that you can combine with the delivery.
- Check if there is enough demand among your customers for a delivery service.
- Consider if there are any suitable partners that you can implement this service with since you don't need your own fleet of delivery agents.

IKEA: Format for City Dwellers

IKEA is the world's largest furniture dealer and was founded in Sweden in 1943 by Ingvar Kamprad, who at the time was 17 years old. Today, the company employs around 211,000 workers. IKEA designs and sells ready-to-assemble furniture, kitchen appliances, and household products at over 400 stores in more than 50 countries.

Image 13.1 IKEA. (Source: UNP photography/IKEA)

IKEA customers in large cities live differently than those in small cities. After all, the living and furnishing requirements are usually different due to the size of the respective living space. In big cities, customers need clever solutions to accommodate all living areas in the smallest possible space. In addition, city dwellers are used to having all their products and services in the immediate vicinity. When buying furniture, for example, they don't need to go to the huge stores at a great distance on the outskirts of the urban areas.

The concept of the "IKEA Planning Studio" is oriented toward the way people in large cities shop at IKEA. The stores are considerably smaller than usual shops and are opened in city centers like in London, New York, Los Angeles, and Chicago. These Planning Studios present smart ideas of how to live in small spaces with IKEA products. In addition, free planning consultation from furnishing experts is offered here that is easy to book online.

Customers don't need to worry about how to get the furniture they have purchased back home using underground transportation, as all products are delivered without exception. There are inclusive prices for unlimited quantities, and delivery occurs even directly into the living room. Home delivery is trouble-free, fast, and inexpensive. In addition to delivery, IKEA offers other services. The time-consuming assembly of products can be taken over as well for a small fee.

IKEA does not have its own fleet of vehicles but instead collaborates with shipping partners like DHL, UPS, and PostNord, who deliver the products worldwide with around 10,000 vehicles. The furniture dealer has undertaken to ensure that by 2025, all deliveries by the cooperation partners will be carried out using more environmentally-friendly electric vehicles.

"IKEA Planning Studios" are completely geared toward the needs of customers. The core offering involves not just products but also a service that is convenient on all levels, a service that covers planning, delivery, and assembly of products.

7-Eleven: Deliver and Care

SEVEN-ELEVEN JAPAN CO., LTD. is a convenience store chain with its headquarters in Tokyo, Japan. The name "7-Eleven" originated in the 1940s, when the opening hours of these shops were from seven o'clock in the morning until eleven o'clock at night. The 7-Eleven brand extends to more than 69,000 convenience stores worldwide in 17 countries. Over 20,000 of these stores are in Japan.

Convenience stores are everywhere in Japan. They are the shops in the neighborhood that offer groceries at reasonable prices. These stores are particularly important for senior citizens, as they can reach them without transportation. This is a strong argument, especially in Japan, where the percentage of the oldest people in the total population is particularly high. Every fourth person is over 65 years of age. 7-Eleven has adapted its products and services accordingly to this target group and offers a delivery service in 70 percent of its stores.

Japanese convenience stores sell a wide range of groceries and everyday items and are located directly in the neighborhoods. In addition to purchases, 7-Eleven also delivers meals to customers. The company ensures that senior citizens can choose nutrition meals with reduced salt content. In order to use this service, you have to be a member of 7-Meal.

Not only online but when visiting the store, customers can order the delivery of these meals in addition to the groceries. In many cases employees of the local store deliver them directly to their homes, which combines a practical delivery with a friendly visit, as these employees have often known their regular customers for many years. Especially for senior citizens who live alone and are often lonely, it is a good feeling for them to see a familiar face in their home.

Home delivery is just the start, however. 7-Eleven is reacting to demographic and other changes in society. This approach even extends to the point that convenience stores are entering into partnerships with local authorities so that 7-Eleven employees can also check the well-being of their elderly customers during daily deliveries. If there is cause for concern, the authorities are informed so that help can be provided.

7-Eleven has recognized that convenience stores are part of the community; they are also part of the solution for challenges associated with aging. 7-Eleven's innovative delivery services set it apart from the competition and online trading, which has a positive effect on business.

Bibliography

Cheng, Andria. 2019. How IKEA Is Using a Small Planning Studio in Manhattan to Drive Its Urban and Online Growth. Forbes. https://www.forbes.com/sites/andriacheng/2019/05/28/ikeas-new-manhattan-planning-studio-spells-growth-and-potentially-missed-opportunities/#1e0061fe640e.

Fehrenbacher, Katie. 2019. How IKEA Plans to Deliver Its Goods Via Electric Trucks and Vans. Green Biz. https://www.greenbiz.com/article/how-ikea-plans-deliver-its-goods-electric-trucks-and-vans.

Ikea. IKEA Planning Studio. https://www.ikea.com/gb/en/stores/planning-studios/.

Stone, Robyn. 2018. What 7-Eleven Can Teach Us About Aging in Community. Global Ageing Network. https://globalageing.org/what-7-eleven-can-teach-us-about-aging-in-community/.

Part IV

Sustainability

The retail business is under closer observation than ever before—by customers. They want to know exactly what a company's position is on sustainability and environmental issues. Who produced the merchandise, where, and under what conditions? What steps is a company taking to operate its stores sustainably? When it comes to environmental friendliness, customers now request absolute transparency, and it increasingly has an influence on purchase decisions. It's good to separate paper from plastic waste and to use environmentally friendly LED lighting in the whole store, but that is far from being enough now. Customers expect more. A lot more.

From the store design, where regional renewable raw materials are used, to the store's energy and water consumption: Recycling, reuse, and waste prevention are important topics that interest consumers. They don't just want to know how a company implements all this; they also want the company to inform them of what they themselves can do to lead a more sustainable life.

But even environmental friendliness in production processes, supply chains, and at the point of sale is still not enough. New strategies are required to extend the products' life cycle, allowing them to be used longer than is the case today. There are a large number of new approaches to this, ranging from rental and subscription models to the resale or repurchase of goods to their preparation.

This chapter will show you how you can meet consumers' expectations when it comes to sustainability. There are many successful examples showing how it works—creatively, innovatively, and always environmentally friendly.

14

Point of Sale

Sustainability in the retail business is and remains a hot topic. But why should retailers focus on sustainability in the first place? On the one hand, of course, for ethical reasons, as it would be nice to know that future generations will still have a planet to call home. On the other hand, it is becoming increasingly important to consumers that companies pursue sustainable business practices. To customers, this is already a central differentiation feature of brands.

Even the store design or window display should reflect sustainability. A first step is to use materials from regional renewable resources. There are already mannequins and coat hangers made entirely of recyclable materials that can also be completely recycled. In addition, sustainable design can also cut costs.

Energy consumption is next on the list. Some companies have solar panels on the roof with which they produce their own electricity. The use of windows and skylights reduces the need for artificial light. This also has the advantage that natural light has a positive effect on people's satisfaction and well-being. The use of LED lighting not only saves electricity but also money.

Use equipment and sanitary facilities that save water. Develop strategies that reduce water consumption both in the production of your goods and for your customers. Encourage consumers, for example, to wash their clothes less often. There are also many regions where air pollution is a major issue and the shopping destination is chosen according to air quality. This may sound surprising, but think of Asia, for example. In some Chinese cities, shopping centers advertise the fact that they are equipped with air purifiers. Displays show the degree of air pollution. Botany can also be used to help: Trees and native plants can be included in the exterior and interior design to improve air quality.

© The Author(s) 2020

M. Spanke, *Retail Isn't Dead*, https://doi.org/10.1007/978-3-030-36650-6_14

Recycling can be implemented in brick-and-mortar retail in many ways, starting with waste being recycled by companies. Or by supplying customers with drop-off points for recyclable materials and clothing donations. Some retailers even take it one step further and opt for pre-cycling, i.e., not generating any waste in the first place. This can involve a whole store without any product packaging or maybe just a section without plastic.

Reuse is a strategy as well that offers retailers new opportunities. For example, by introducing reusable bags or product packaging. Beauty brands offer customers a discount if they bring empty containers back for refilling. This is already being successfully implemented with fragrance bottles, creams, and hand detergents.

Consumers want to reduce waste, refill, and recycle, but they are not always sure how. Through in-store communication or workshops, retailers can show their customers how it works. Offer discounts when recyclable products are returned or reusable containers are refilled. Not only does this help the environment, but it also increases customer frequency and confidence in you. After all, it gives consumers a good feeling to know that a company doesn't just think about profit but about the environment as well.

Call to Action

- Use recyclable materials and regional renewable resources for your store and window design.
- Find ways to reduce energy and water consumption. Try to prevent waste, to recycle, and to reuse items in all business areas.
- Show customers through in-store communication and workshops how to live sustainably. Communicate your sustainable actions at the store, on your website, and on social media.
- Develop a customer loyalty program that rewards environmentally friendly purchasing behavior.

BOTTLETOP: Store Design Printed by a Robot

BOTTLETOP was founded in 2002 for a design collaboration with the British accessory brand Mulberry. The company focuses on the use of upcycling materials for sustainably manufactured luxury handbags. Hence the company name BOTTLETOP—the first bag collection was made from these. The BOTTLETOP

FOUNDATION, which is at the heart of the company, supports young people in Ethiopia, Kenya, Malawi, Mozambique, Rwanda, Zimbabwe, Brazil, and Great Britain through health education programs. The company currently runs a store in London. With its products, BOTTLETOP is represented by various multi-label luxury suppliers.

Image 14.1 BOTTLETOP. (Source: Andrew Meredith)

The *BOTTLETOP* brand stands for sustainable luxury, ethical design, technical innovation, and intercultural collaboration. These values and orientation are decisive for all manufacturing processes related to the collections. It goes without saying that the *BOTTLETOP* flagship store on Regent Street in London in particular should consistently meet these requirements. Sustainability starts with the collection and continues in the store design. In this case, the latter means environmentally responsible building through waste-free design.

The interior of the London store evolved over a time period of two months. Business continued during this time so that customers could experience up close the recycling process and the resulting generation of something new. The store walls consist of a repetitive three-dimensional pattern. It was formed in sight of customers with a 3D printing robot and consists entirely of recycled plastic bottles. The raw material was first washed, crushed, extruded, and prepared so it could be used for the unique store design. Upon completion, 60,000 recycled plastic bottles had been reused.

The ceiling of the store consists of a metal roof with thousands of cans embedded in a suspended 3D-printed grid structure. The floor is made of worn bicycle tires. Thus, absolutely all areas of the store are built with ecological responsibility and without waste.

For the limited time of the store's evolution, customers were able to interact with the robot. They also received personalized *BOTTLETOP* bag pendants that were printed with the plastic filament. Visitors thus experienced the sustainability and innovation of *BOTTLETOP* at first hand while shopping and learned more about the ecological background of the company's mission.

IKEA: Sustainability Record on the Thames

IKEA is the world's largest furniture dealer and was founded in Sweden in 1943 by Ingvar Kamprad, who at the time was 17 years old. Today, the company employs around 211,000 workers. IKEA designs and sells ready-to-assemble furniture, kitchen appliances, and household products at over 400 stores in more than 50 countries.

Image 14.2   IKEA. (Source: IKEA)

At IKEA, sustainability is not just a catchphrase but an integral part of the corporate philosophy. With the opening of the store in the London district of Greenwich, new standards were set in terms of sustainability, and not only with regards to design and architecture. The local community was supposed to be encouraged to lead a healthier and more sustainable lifestyle. In 2019 IKEA Greenwich was officially ranked the most sustainable store in Great Britain.

The whole store consists entirely of renewable resources. 99 percent of the site's non-hazardous construction waste was recycled. Most of the roof area is covered with solar panels to supply the building with electricity. Thanks to the consistent use of glass and skylights, a lot of daylight enters the interior, which is why there is hardly any need for LED-based artificial light. During the winter months, the store is heated with an environmentally friendly geothermal heating system, and through the use of rainwater, only half of the usual water consumption is necessary.

There is a terrace on the roof of the building with enough space for up to 500 people. It has a rooftop garden with specially selected plants that purify the air to a great extent. In addition to this area, which is accessible to customers and employees, there are other rooms for flexible use where yoga or meditation courses and various workshops are offered.

IKEA Greenwich also has a variety of courses to inform consumers on how they can lead a more sustainable life, without having to completely turn their lives upside down. In the workshops, experts share their knowledge on how to reduce waste, repair or redesign furniture, reuse textiles, and much more.

What could be closer to sustainability than thinking of the younger generation? That's why IKEA works closely with local schools, allowing specialist knowledge on growth, nutrition, and energy conservation to be passed on to children. This teaches them to limit themselves to what they really need—whether in food, water, or energy. In addition, IKEA supports wildlife in the neighborhood by funding a nearby ecology park.

And that's not all: The store is located in such a way that customers can reach it easily and environmentally friendly—by bike, on foot, and even by boat. There are numerous bicycle stands in front of the building.

With energy conservation, recycling, and upcycling, IKEA Greenwich is not only a role model for the local community but also for physical retailers all over the world. More sustainability is hardly possible.

Original Unverpackt: Fill It Yourself at the Supermarket

Original Unverpackt GmbH [Original Unpackaged LLC] is a German retail business that opened in Berlin in 2014. The store offers around 600 different products. These include grain products, muesli, sauces, oil, pasta, spices, teas, toothpaste, shampoo, conditioner, cosmetics, cleaning agents, and much more. The distinctive feature is that in the zero waste store—as the name implies—everything is sold without subsequent waste, i.e., without any packaging. The team from Original Unverpackt consists of 20 employees.

Image 14.3   Original Unverpackt. (Source: Original Unverpackt, Katja Vogt)

Today, almost all everyday items from toothpaste to muesli have packaging. Sometimes they even have additional packaging within the packaging. If we were all to do without the packaging waste of our everyday products, then this small step would already have tremendous effects. This is exactly the concept of Original Unverpackt. There is not a single package to be seen in the entire store. Instead, all the products are available in large dispensers for filling.

Those who want to make a purchase bring their own containers or bottles from home that can be used over and over again. They then have these containers weighed, whereupon a small label with the respective weight specification is applied to them. Whoever prefers not to have a label acquires reusable containers from Original Unverpackt that do not have to be weighed for future purchases. Then you can start. Only the amounts that you need are filled—no matter how much or how little that is. The containers are weighed at the checkout, the weight specified on the label is subtracted, and the filled merchandise is paid for. Everything is calculated by weight. Since the price of the packaging is normally calculated into the price of the product, the products here are usually even cheaper as well.

Original Unverpackt is plastic-free throughout the entire supply chain, and with paper, every effort is made to keep material waste as low as possible. Goods are delivered primarily by local organic companies in order to avoid unnecessary environmental impacts. Since the goods don't have any packaging, there is no branding, i.e., no logo, no pictures, and no typical brand colors. As unusual as this may seem, customers don't mind it.

In addition, there is an online shop for non-food products. No plastic is used for the delivery service, and the solution for its packaging is upcycling, i.e., the reuse of boxes.

All corporate decisions at Original Unverpackt are always made with sustainability in mind. The intention here is to convey to the public that it is actually quite easy to reduce waste and live sustainably. And this experience is precisely what the team passes on to its customers in daily business.

Ekoplaza: "Plastic-Free Aisle"

The organic market chain Ekoplaza was founded in 1999 and has its headquarters in Veghel in the Netherlands. The company has more than 80 supermarkets in the Netherlands.

Image 14.4 Ekoplaza. (Source: Ekoplaza)

Plastic waste is a serious and growing concern among the population worldwide. Finally, even politicians are alarmed. Rightly so, of course, because plastic waste causes enormous damage in oceans and is a danger to the food chain. However, microplastics and toxic plastic additives don't only reach "our plates" through the seas and fish but also through insects and birds. In other words, plastic is inside us. The food retail business accounts for an enormous percentage of plastic packaging used worldwide. Therefore, Ekoplaza 2018 initiated a concept that makes it easier for customers to reduce their plastic footprint. The company opened the world's first supermarket aisle without plastic, the so-called "Plastic Free Aisle."

Around 700 everyday products are offered here, ranging from rice, milk, chocolate, yogurt, fruit, and vegetables to sauces, meat, and much more. Everything is supplied in glass, metal, cardboard, or biofilm. Biofilm is plant-based and can be composted. It is made of cellulose, wood pulp, algae, grass, cornstarch, shrimp shells, and the like.

The idea of drastically reduced waste in the food retail business is nothing new. There are now numerous zero waste stores where goods are filled into containers brought by customers. The big difference between this system and the plastic-free aisle is that Ekoplaza matches consumers' normal shopping behavior more closely with its concept. Here, there is no need to bring containers and to fill and weigh any goods. Thus, it is a much easier step in the transition to shopping with reduced waste.

As a grocery chain, Ekoplaza has managed to multiply its sustainability strategy with a branch concept of supermarkets.

Bibliography

Arthur, Rachel. 2017. London Store Upcycles 60,000 Plastic Bottles Into 3D-Printed Interior. *Forbes*. https://www.forbes.com/sites/rachelarthur/2017/12/07/london-store-upcycles-60000-plastic-bottles-into-3d-printed-interior/#728973f5777f.

BRE Group. 2019. IKEA Greenwich Achieves Highest BREEAM UK New Construction Sustainability Rating. https://www.bregroup.com/press-releases/ikea-greenwich-achieve-highest-breeam-uk-new-construction-sustainability-rating/.

Bretschkow, Antonia. 2018. Neuer "Unverpackt"-Laden in Prenzlauer Berg. *Der Tagesspiegel*. https://www.tagesspiegel.de/berlin/abfallvermeidung-in-berlin-neuer-unverpackt-laden-in-prenzlauer-berg/21248310.html.

Brutscher, Fiona. 2018. Goodbye Garbage: Packaging-Free Supermarkets and the Zero-Waste Life. *American Express*. https://www.amexessentials.com/packaging-free-supermarkets/.

Ekoplaza. Ekoplaza Lab. https://www.ekoplaza.nl/pagina/ekoplaza-lab-1.

Ikea. 2019. Welcome to the World's Most Sustainable IKEA Store. https://www.ikea.com/gb/en/ideas/welcome-to-the-worlds-most-sustainable-ikea-store-pub76f14481.

Taylor, Matthew. 2018. World's First Plastic-Free Aisle Opens in Netherlands Supermarket. *The Guardian*. https://www.theguardian.com/environment/2018/feb/28/worlds-first-plastic-free-aisle-opens-in-netherlands-supermarket.

Valentine, Matthew. 2018. Design Showcase: 3D Printed Store Interior for Bottletop. *Retail Design World*. https://retaildesignworld.com/news/design-showcase-3d-printed-store/.

15

Rent, Resale, Redesign

Market development towards fast fashion has contributed to the fact that the technical life span of clothing is completely disproportionate to its practical life span. This means that technically, almost every article of clothing can be worn much longer than it actually is. Younger consumers in particular are demanding strategies to extend the active life of garments. So far, most sustainability efforts in retail have focused on an environmentally friendly production and supply chain. But this is no longer sufficient for consumers. Thank goodness. Against this background, new concepts have been developed that meet these demands and are positively received by customers.

Nowadays, there are subscription and rental models for just about all consumption sectors, from vehicles or furniture to clothes or accessories. They're not just in the luxury and premium segment but now all across the board, for customers' behavior in relation to renting goods has changed. In the past, you would have only borrowed an outfit from your best friend, but now, even this has become a successful business model.

Resale programs are no longer niche strategies, either, as the number of customers who want to involve sustainability in their purchase decisions is steadily increasing. With pop-up areas for vintage and second-hand goods, even established brands can test this sector for themselves. This has great potential: If implemented correctly, customer frequency is increased, the target group is extended, and high-priced brands can also introduce customers with lower purchasing power to their own brand.

© The Author(s) 2020
M. Spanke, *Retail Isn't Dead*, https://doi.org/10.1007/978-3-030-36650-6_15

Buying back your own merchandise also presents advantages for you and your customers. A good strategy should ensure that the merchandise returned is put to sensible continued use and offer the participating customer a bonus program. If consumers return a garment, then they could receive a voucher, for example. That way, you not only draw customers to your store but also increase the chances that they return home with new purchases.

Processing or repairing goods is another topic with which you can inspire customers. Workshops or events enhance your company's sustainable image and encourage strong customer loyalty.

The rapid growth of rental and resale models clearly shows that this strategy has a future. The advantages for the customer are obvious: There is a better price-performance ratio, and customers get the opportunity to own market products that they might not be able to afford otherwise. At the same time, there is a growing desire for products to be handled in a more sustainable manner by extending their useful life.

Call to Action

- Consider which of the following possibilities constitute an advantage for your customers and are highly likely to be used: renting, reselling, repurchasing, or processing your products.
- Once you have chosen one or more of these possibilities, define how the procedure for such a concept should look so it can be integrated into your business processes.
- During this process, don't lose sight of the idea of sustainability. Make sure that this is an important point when communicating your strategy outwards.

ba&sh: Free Choice in the "Dream Closet"

ba&sh is a French premium fashion brand that sells apparel, bags, accessories, and shoes at affordable prices. The company, which was founded in 2003, has its headquarters in Paris. Currently, it has over 200 stores. The majority of these stores are in France. In addition, the collections are distributed internationally at premium department stores and on the internet. The target group involves women of all ages who have a feminine and comfortable fashion style.

Image 15.1 ba&sh. (Source: ba&sh)

"The Dream Closet" is an experiment that allows ba&sh customers at the New York store to help themselves on a whim to items from a "Dream Closet." This is almost as if you were to borrow an outfit from your best friend for the weekend. However, the selection here is much, much larger and usually more luxurious.

The "Dream Closet" concept perfectly fits the modern lifestyle of New York women for whom a "sharing economy" is becoming more and more important. This means borrowing or renting clothes and other items instead of always having to own everything at once. The popularity of the borrowing-culture is certainly also due to the growing dispute on a sustainable lifestyle. After all, this involves products from all sectors, from furnishing to electric scooters to apparel, that are used together with other people.

This is how it works at the ba&sh store in the New York suburb of SoHo: Every Friday at happy hour, customers can borrow items for special occasions free of charge, provided they return them by 7pm on Monday. The credit card number is left behind as security, although the credit card is not charged. So far, it has worked wonderfully: All the garments are returned in perfect condition.

Providing the clothes for free allows customers to discover the brand more easily. Thus, younger shoppers have been successfully introduced to the brand, and some customers who have borrowed items have turned into buying customers thanks to "The Dream Closet."

American Eagle Outfitters: Rental Subscription for Outfits

American Eagle Outfitters, Inc. is an American lifestyle apparel and accessories chain with its headquarters in Pittsburgh, Pennsylvania. The company, which was founded in 1977, employs 40,000 workers and has more than 1200 stores worldwide. The stores, which average 5300 square feet in size, offer fashionable apparel, accessories, and care products to their target group of female and male students. The average age of their customers is between 15 and 25.

Customers have changed their consumer behavior. Rentals and resales have become a large fashion trend, as younger customers in particular are looking for new consumption models, which include sustainable shopping possibilities. American Eagle satisfies exactly this customer need with the rental model "American Eagle Style Drop," a rental subscription for apparel. For 49.95 dollars a month, customers can rent three items at once and swap these as often as they like. If they want to keep one of these articles, they even receive a discount. Shipping costs and cleaning are included in the monthly fee. This is obviously an attractive package, as the model is enthusiastically accepted.

American Eagle even has a special strategy when it comes to resale. It has entered into a partnership with the popular resale brand Urban Necessities. The Las Vegas-based company specializes in the resale of popular sneakers. These now complement the American Eagle assortment. The collection includes sneakers that are sold at prices between 150 and 50,000 dollars. Self-lacing Nike shoes like those featured in the movie "Back to the Future" can be found here, for example.

In the New York suburb of SoHo, a pop-up has been opened that covers an area of 1900 square feet. The combination of trendy denim and cool sneakers is perfect, especially as the articles do not compete with each other but complement each other. Even if both companies have different price categories, the brands themselves are not too dissimilar. After all, four out of ten Urban Necessities customers wear American Eagle products.

Further locations are already planned for this new partnership. It is so promising that American Eagle has even acquired a stake in the sneaker resale dealer Urban Necessities. This enables American Eagle to continually expand its consumer base and increase customer frequency at its own stores.

REI: "Used Gear Swap"—Exchange Platform for Outdoor Fans

Recreational Equipment, Inc., commonly known as REI, is an American outdoor retail company. Founded in 1938, REI has its headquarters in Kent, in the state of Washington. Over 150 stores offer customers sporting goods, camping and travel gear, and apparel. Services such as travel and outdoor courses complete the offer. Currently, more than 13,000 employees work for the company. The target group involves men and women who range from occasional outdoor fans to experienced adventurers.

Sustainability is part of REI's corporate strategy. As a result, the specialist retailer for outdoor equipment has expanded its sales programs for borrowed and used equipment as well as its exchange options. Starting with exchange platforms at the stores, the sustainability initiative was further extended. After all, renting and reselling not only save money but help keep products from prematurely ending up in landfills. And that, in turn, is a big step toward transitioning to a circular economy.

With the ongoing commitment to sustainability, REI stores regularly organize "Used Gear Swaps", so-called exchange and purchase platforms. Here, members can bring their discarded and well preserved outdoor equipment to other users. The events are free of charge for REI members. Lifelong membership is covered with a one-time payment of 20 dollars. Here, you can find everything your outdoor heart desires, from bicycles, skis, boats, tents, and backpacks to flashlights. Those who aren't able to be present at the "Used Gear Swap" in person can buy the used equipment online. "Re-Commerce" is the name of the concept. REI has even developed its own website for the resale of used products at affordable prices.

Renting equipment is yet another one of the company's sustainability initiatives. Most of the REI locations offer a service for ski boots, skis, snowboards, and complete sets of camping and backpacking gear to rent.

It doesn't matter whether something is for resale or for rent—the business is good and sustainable, and REI has shown that it can also be successful.

Eileen Fisher: Test Site for Upcycling

Eileen Fisher is an American fashion designer and founder of the eponymous retail company Eileen Fisher Inc. In 1986, two years after founding the company, she opened her first store in Manhattan, New York. Today, her women's fashion, accessories, and shoes are represented at 62 stores and around 1000 department and specialty stores internationally. The company employs over 1200 workers. Eileen Fisher's primary target group involves women ranging in age from 35 to 55.

Image 15.2 Eileen Fisher. (Source: Eileen Fisher)

"Renew" is the name of Eileen Fisher's innovative strategy. Her mission: The company itself should demonstrate sustainability and thereby inspire customers toward a more environmentally compatible lifestyle. The fashion brand manages to do so time and again with ambitious initiatives.

The "Renew" program was already developed years ago in order to extend the life cycle of garments. The concept stipulates wearing the merchandise as long as you like, then passing it on to someone else. This is how it works: If a customer brings an Eileen Fisher garment back to a store, she receives a five-dollar voucher that can be redeemed at any of the stores. From there, everything is sent to one of the two recycling centers in Seattle, Washington or Irvington, New York. There, the merchandise is checked for wear, stains, and holes, as only garments that are in perfect condition are resold. The rest is processed into pieces of art made of felt. The garments that were selected for resale are cleaned through an environmentally friendly process and resold at affordable prices at the online shop and at select Eileen Fisher stores. Since

2009, over 1.3 million garments have been returned, setting a new standard in sustainability for retail companies.

Eileen Fisher's Brooklyn store is their latest sustainability innovation. In the New York district of Brooklyn, a store has been created on an area of 4900 square feet where the DNA of the fashion brand is reflected. Here, it's not just about selling the current collection, although that, too, has its place here. It's more about making the brand's values visible and sensitizing the community for a sustainable treatment of clothing. It is a true test site with exclusive collections, community events, and much more.

In the interior and exterior of the store, customers can relax, engage in handicrafts, or participate in one of the many events. There are public workshops for mending, sewing, and washing the clothes to prolong their life. Events with guest speakers and panel discussions complement the concept, all geared toward customers interested in sustainability and extending the life cycle of garments.

The store employees here are so-called "Guides." Their main task is to build personal relationships with the customers and to convey the company's values to them. They provide tips and suggestions that help everyone live more sustainably. Eileen Fisher shows us that environmentally friendly strategies such as upcycling with "zero waste" can be very cool and stylish.

Bibliography

Ba&sh. Dream Store. https://ba-sh.com/us/nolita-store.html.

Cheng, Andria. 2019. American Eagle Puts Its Best Foot Forward with Gen Z, Unveiling a Sneaker Resale Shop. *Forbes*. https://www.forbes.com/sites/andriacheng/2019/03/08/american-eagle-urban-necessities/#780c1f393876.

Edelson, Sharon. 2018. Experience Matters: A New Eileen Fisher Retail Concept Grows in Brooklyn. *WWD*. https://wwd.com/business-news/retail/experience-matters-a-new-eileen-fisher-retail-concept-grows-in-brooklyn-1202775211/.

Eileen Fisher. Eileen Fisher Renew. https://www.eileenfisherrenew.com/our-story.

Hughes, Huw. 2018. French Label Ba&sh Allows Customers to Borrow Clothes for Free in New York Store. Fashion United. https://fashionunited.uk/news/retail/french-label-ba-sh-allows-customers-to-borrow-clothes-for-free-in-new-york-store/2018101939547.

REI Co-op. 2018. REI Co-op Continues Commitment to Sustainability by Hosting 11 Used Gear Swaps Across the Country on Oct. 27. https://newsroom.rei.com/news/corporate/rei-co-op-continues-commitment-to-sustainability-by-hosting-11-used-gear-swaps-across-country-on-oct-27.htm.

Verry, Peter. 2019. 'Why Urban Necessities' New Store in American Eagle Is the Answer to 'Broken' Retail. *Footwear News*. https://footwearnews.com/2019/business/retail/urban-necessities-new-york-city-store-american-eagle-1202759093/.

16

Closing Words

RETAIL ISN'T DEAD—not offline and definitely not online. But what does the future hold? What developments are emerging today for the physical retail of tomorrow?

There are signs that soon, every customer will be able to be located anywhere and at any time in a store. This will make it possible to offer consumers a completely personalized shopping experience. Convenience and service will certainly continue to be extended further. Especially in sectors that are recurring and may not be a lot of fun: Will even groceries and cleaning agents soon be purchased and delivered automatically?

Speed and immediate availability require a networked inventory. Not only will your stores and online shop be able to access everything, but maybe also every retailer and even every customer worldwide. Will checkouts soon be a thing of the past? Will just about all stores soon be part of the so-called "Third Places", that is, "Intermediate Places," which in addition to work and home are places for gathering, relaxing, and experiences?

Some of these scenarios are already a reality. But how do we know today already what our customers want tomorrow? Which technological innovations should we prepare for as early as possible to drive solutions for our retail situations?

Follow trend developments and be open to new things, not just occasionally but all the time. Analyze information and data in order to make sound predictions. After all, data will be one of the most decisive, if not even the most decisive, success factors for retail.

Ask your customers what they like about your store and especially what they don't like. What are customers missing? These weaknesses are your

M. Spanke, *Retail Isn't Dead*, https://doi.org/10.1007/978-3-030-36650-6_16

window of opportunity. Develop strategies that in a creative and innovative way are tailored to your customers and even to each and every one individually.

During all this, you should always be aware of one thing: Tomorrow's new strategy will already be yesterday's strategy by the time the day after tomorrow arrives.

There is, however, a timeless strategy for success: customer satisfaction.

Matthias Spanke
Chief Executive Officer of BIG IDEAS Visual Merchandising Inc,
United States
Chief Executive Officer of BIG IDEAS Visual Merchandising GmbH, Germany
Chief Executive Officer of BIG CAREERS Retail Recruitment, Germany

BIG IDEAS Visual Merchandising

BIG IDEAS Visual Merchandising is backed by a team of international retail and visual merchandising experts. The full-service agency offers retailers from around the world an all-round service from strategy development to design and production to global roll-out. Always with the objective of offering end customers an unforgettable brand experience and generating a significant increase in sales for clients.

BIG IDEAS has offices in Europe and the US and serves a variety of renowned international brands.

© The Author(s) 2020
M. Spanke, *Retail Isn't Dead*, https://doi.org/10.1007/978-3-030-36650-6

Within the framework of its retail consulting services, BIG IDEAS advises and supports brands to ensure a perfect customer experience at the point of sale. During this process, BIG IDEAS not only assumes the creative direction of innovative window and in-store concepts but also the production and global delivery. Visual merchandising directives are developed to transfer the concepts to every point of sale in an optimal way. Upon request, this is also possible in the form of virtual reality directives.

With its visual merchandising field support, BIG IDEAS makes it possible to implement window and in-store concepts worldwide. The global team consists of local visual merchandising experts who simultaneously deal with the success and visual appearance of the brands. With offices on two continents and in different time zones, BIG IDEAS is almost always available for its customers.

BIG IDEAS also offers presentations, workshops, and training to inspire participants of conferences and corporate events with the latest trends and to expand their know-how on topics like retail trends, retail experience, or visual merchandising.

Would you like to find out more? The team at BIG IDEAS looks forward to hearing from you.

Web: www.big-ideas.com
Email: info@big-ideas.com

BIG CAREERS Retail Recruitment

BIG CAREERS is an agency specialized on the recruitment of retail professionals from corporate and creative to sales experts. Based on a long-term commitment to the retail industry the BIG CAREERS team will find the right fit at every level for professionals.

Visual merchandising experts, store managers, area managers, sales directors or any other talents: Would you like to find out how we bring your brand together with the best professionals?

Web: www.big-careers.com
Email: hello@big-careers.com

© The Author(s) 2020
M. Spanke, *Retail Isn't Dead*, https://doi.org/10.1007/978-3-030-36650-6

Index

© The Author(s) 2020
M. Spanke, *Retail Isn't Dead*, https://doi.org/10.1007/978-3-030-36650-6

Printed by Printforce, the Netherlands